AIRCAM/**AIRWAR** SERIES   EDITOR: MARTIN WINDROW

USAAF MEDIUM BOMBER UNITS
ETO AND MTO, 1942-45

BY RENÉ J. FRANÇILLON

COLOUR PLATES BY
TOM BRITTAIN AND
GERRY EMBLETON

OSPREY PUBLISHING LONDON

Published in 1977 by
Osprey Publishing Ltd
Member company of the George Philip Group
12–14 Long Acre, London WC2E 9LP
© Copyright 1977 Osprey Publishing Ltd

ISBN 0 85045 205 8

Filmset by BAS Printers Limited, Wallop, Hampshire, England
Printed in Hong Kong

USAAF MEDIUM BOMBER UNITS, ETO AND MTO 1942-45

PRELUDE

Whereas in 1941 the fighter aircraft of the newly organized United States Army Air Forces were markedly inferior to those flown by the major fighting powers, the USAAF had already introduced into squadron service four of the most famous bomber aircraft of the Second World War. These included the Boeing B-17 Flying Fortress, which in its first fully combat-worthy form (B-17E) had been delivered during the autumn of 1941 to the 7th Bombardment Group, and three of the four types of light and medium bombers which were flown in combat until VE-Day: the Martin B-26 Marauder and North American B-25 Mitchell had first entered service in 1941, with the 22nd and 17th Bombardment Groups (Medium) respectively, whilst the Douglas A-20 Havoc had first been delivered earlier during the same year to the 3rd Bombardment Group (Light).

In December 1941, when the United States was forced into the war by Japanese aggression, the USAAF comprised 71 groups, including 14 light and medium bomber groups which were flying a variety of aircraft in addition to the new A-20s, B-25s and B-26s. Of the seven Bombardment Groups (Light) then available only two went on to fight as light bomber units: the 3rd BG operated in the Pacific with the Fifth Air Force and the 47th BG joined the Twelfth Air Force in North Africa. The 12th BG (L) became a medium bomber unit prior to joining the Ninth Air Force in the Western Desert, the 27th and 48th were successively redesignated as Bombardment Groups (Dive), Fighter-Bomber Groups and finally Fighter Groups, and the 45th and 46th BGs (L) remained in the United States. Four of the seven prewar Bombardment Groups (Medium), the 22nd, 38th, 41st and 42nd, fought in the Pacific, the 17th BG (M) served with the Twelfth Air Force in North Africa and the Mediterranean, the 40th served in the

Caribbean prior to being trained as a B-29 unit, and the 13th BG (M) was deactivated in the United States during November 1942. To supplement these prewar units, the USAAF activated seven bombardment groups (Light) and sixteen bombardment groups (Medium) during 1942 and 1943. Eight of the prewar and wartime light and medium bombardment groups served in the Western Desert, North Africa and Mediterranean Theatre of Operations (MTO) between August 1942 and May 1945 whilst eleven of these units operated in the European Theatre of Operations (ETO).

NINTH AIR FORCE IN THE WESTERN DESERT

Though Germany was recognized by the Western Allies as their most powerful enemy, and therefore their primary target, the United States had no choice during the first months of the war but to deploy most of her initially weak forces to contain the Japanese onslaught in the Pacific and south-east Asia. However, in June 1942, twenty-three Consolidated B-24Ds which had been ferried across the South Atlantic and Africa on their way to China had to be retained in Egypt to help stop the advance of the *Afrika Korps* towards the Suez Canal. Thus, this small force, which was known as the Halverson Detachment (after the name of its CO, Col. Henry A. Halverson), became the first American unit to serve with the newly organized United States Army Middle East Air Force (USAMEAF). Shortly thereafter this meagre force was bolstered by the arrival of the 12th BG (B-25Cs), 57th FG (Curtiss P-40Fs) and 98th BG (B-24Ds). To reach the combat zone the crews of the 12th BG ferried their aircraft from

1. The 111th Observation Squadron, a Texas National Guard unit, was called to active duty on 25 November 1940. Two years later it arrived in North Africa for Operation *Torch*, flying A-20Bs; the Havocs were used mainly for anti-submarine and reconnaissance missions. Squadron insignia was a gold star pierced by the Ace of Diamonds. (Texas ANG)

Morrison Field, Florida to Egypt via the South Atlantic and across Africa, the first aircraft leaving Florida on 14 July, and the last arriving in Egypt on 11 August 1942. Five days after the last aircraft had arrived, the group flew its first night mission against Mersa Matruh, and two weeks later it was thrown into full-scale operations alongside No. 3 Wing, South African Air Force, to support ground forces in the battle of El Alamein. Despite its lack of sufficient operational training, the 12th BG performed its tasks successfully whilst attacking ground targets, airfields and harbours. In so doing, the group began moving to forward bases to follow the British Eighth Army which was rapidly pushing the

Afrika Korps westward into Cyrenaica and Tripolitania, and by mid-December 1942 it was based at airfields around Gambut, Cyrenaica; by then the parent organization of the 12th BG, the USAMEAF, had been re-organized into the Ninth Air Force.

January 1943 saw the 12th BG continuing to support the advance of the British ground forces—Tripoli was captured on the 23rd of that month and Rommel's forces retreated into Tunisia to take a defensive position along the Mareth Line—and, for the first time, it bombed a target outside Africa: airfields on the island of Crete which were struck on 2 January. During the following month the group was split into two when its 81st and 82nd BSs moved to Berteaux, Algeria, to operate under the control of the Twelfth Air Force, whilst its 83rd and 434th BSs remained with the Ninth Air Force. However, on the last day of the following month these last-mentioned squadrons were reinforced by some aircraft and crews of the 340th BG. This unit,

2. A-20B-DL, 41-3491, of the 47th BG (Light) sharing waterlogged Italian airfield with Spitfire LF Mk IXs of Nos. 93 and 225 Sqns, RAF, and P-47Ds of the 325th FG. Note airscoop above cowling which identified the A-20B version. (USAF)

which had arrived in Egypt a few days earlier, after ferrying its Mitchells from the United States, flew its first group missions on 19 April 1943. Operating from bases in Tripolitania and southern Tunisia, the six B-25 squadrons of the 12th and 340th BGs, together with the Algeria-based A-20, B-25 and B-26 units of the Twelfth Air Force, then concentrated their efforts on smashing the last offensive of the *Afrika Korps* and then on impeding the enemy attempts to withdraw its remaining forces to Sicily and Italy.

As the African campaign came to an end, the 12th and 340th BGs switched their attention to the Italian bases in the Pelagie islands (Pantelleria, Lampedusa, Lampione and Linosa) and first bombed Pantelleria on 8th May 1943. The success of this air assault was evident when, on 11 June, Pantelleria was invaded without opposition. The next objective of the Allied offensive in the Mediterranean, Sicily, required a more costly operation which for the Mitchell groups of the Ninth Air Force began immediately after the fall of Pantelleria when pre-invasion strikes were flown. Operating from Hergla, Tunisia, the 12th and

USAAF MEDIUM & LIGHT BOMBER GROUPS AND THEIR AIRCRAFT, NORTH AFRICA, MTO & ETO, 1942–45

Key: A-20 Havoc (−) B-25 Mitchell (*) B-26 Marauder (+) A-26 Invader (=)

Date / Unit	1942 J	A	S	O	N	D	1943 J	F	M	A	M	J	J	A	S	O	N	D	1944 J	F	M	A	M	J	J	A	S	O	N	D	1945 J	F	M	A	M
N. Africa & MTO																																			
12th BG (M)	(9th AF)	*	*	*	*	*	*	*	*	*	*	*	*	(to 12th AF) *	*	*	*	*	*	(to 10th AF, CBI)															
17th BG (M)	(12th AF)						+	+	+	+	+	+	+	+	+	+	+	+	+	+	+	+	+	+	+	+	+	+	+	+	(to 1st TAF-P) +	+	+	+	+
47th BG (L)	(12th AF)	−	−	−	−	−	−	−	−	−	−	−	−	−	−	−	−	−	−	−	−	−	−	−	−	−	−	−	−	−	− &/=	&/=	&/=	&/=	&/=
310th BG (M)	(12th AF)	*	*	*	*	*	*	*	*	*	*	*	*	*	*	*	*	*	*	*	*	*	*	*	*	*	*	*	*	*	*	*	*	*	*
319th BG (M)	(12th AF)	+	+	+	+	+	+	+	+	+	+	+	+	+	+	+	+	+	+	+	+	+	+	+	+	+	+	+	+	+	* (to USA)				
320th BG (M)	(12th AF)					+	+	+	+	+	+	+	+	+	+	+	+	+	+	+	+	+	+	+	+	+	+	+	+	+	(to 1st TAF-P) +	+	+	+	+
321st BG (M)	(12th AF)				*	*	*	*	*	*	*	*	*	*	*	*	*	*	*	*	*	*	*	*	*	*	*	*	*	*	*	*	*	*	*
340th BG (M)	(9th AF)				*	*	*	*	*(to 12th AF)	*	*	*	*	*	*	*	*	*	*	*	*	*	*	*	*	*	*	*	*	*	*	*	*	*	*
ETO																																			
322nd BG (M)							(8th AF)		+	+	+	+	+	(to 9th AF)	+	+	+	+	+	+	+	+	+	+	+	+	+	+	+	+	+	+	+	+	+
323rd BG (M)							(8th AF)					+	+	+	(to 9th AF) +	+	+	+	+	+	+	+	+	+	+	+	+	+	+	+	+	+	+	+
344th BG (M)														(9th AF)					+	+	+	+	+	+	+	+	+	+	+	+	+	+	+	+	+
386th BG (M)										(8th AF)		+	+	(to 9th AF) +	+	+	+	+	+	+	+	+	+	+	+	+	+	+	+	+	+	=	=	=
387th BG (M)										(8th AF)		+	+	(to 9th AF) +	+	+	+	+	+	+	+	+	+	+	+	+	+	+	+	+	+	+	+	+
391st BG (M)														(9th AF) +	+	+	+	+	+	+	+	+	+	+	+	+	+	+	+	+	=	=
394th BG (M)															(9th AF)		+	+	+	+	+	+	+	+	+	+	+	+	+	+	+	+
397th BG (M)															(9th AF)			+	+	+	+	+	+	+	+	+	+	+	+	+	+	+
409th BG (L)															(9th AF)		−	−	−	−	−	−	−	−	−	=	=	=	=	=
410th BG (L)															(9th AF)		−	−	−	−	−	−	−	−	−	−	−	−	−	=
416th BG (L)															(9th AF)		−	−	−	−	−	−	−	−	−	=	=	=	=	=
Groups in N. Afr/MTO	0	1	1	1	2	5	5	5	6	8	8	8	8	8	8	8	8	8	8	7	7	7	7	7	7	7	7	7	7	7	6	6	6	6	6
Groups in ETO	0	0	0	0	0	0	0	0	0	0	1	1	3	4	4	4	4	4	5	5	8	10	11	11	11	11	11	11	11	11	11	11	11	11	11
Total of groups	0	1	1	1	2	5	5	5	6	8	9	9	11	12	12	12	12	12	13	12	15	17	18	18	18	18	18	18	18	18	17	17	17	17	17

340th BGs flew day and night missions in support of American and British troops which had landed in Sicily on 10 July, and bombed bridges, roads and other communication facilities. Beginning during the first week of August, bases of operations were moved to Sicily with the 12th being stationed at Gela Ponte Olivo whilst the 340th went to Comiso. Messina was captured on 17 August thus bringing to an end the invasion of Sicily. The capture of this island also ended the Mediterranean campaign of the Ninth Air Force, as it was transferred, without air units, to England to become the US Tactical Air Force in Northern Europe; its 12th and 340th BGs were re-assigned to the Twelfth Air Force, and thus remained in the MTO.

TWELFTH AIR FORCE IN NORTH AFRICA AND SOUTHERN EUROPE

In order to provide air support for the American and British troops which were to land at three points on the Atlantic and Mediterranean coasts of North Africa, on 8 November 1942, as part of Operation *Torch,* the USAAF activated the Twelfth Air Force on 20 August 1942. Initially the newly established Twelfth Air Force obtained two-thirds of its strength from the Eighth Air Force, from which was transferred an independent light bomber squadron and thirteen groups, including heavy bomber, fighter, transport and reconnaissance units, then based in England; whilst the balance was provided by eight additional groups directly assigned from the United States. Two of these groups, the 47th BG (L) and the 68th Observation Group, were equipped with Douglas A-20 light bombers whilst the 310th

and 321st BGs (M) had North American B-25Cs, and the 17th, 319th and 320th BGs (M) flew Martin B-26Bs. However, the 68th Observation Group was to see only limited operations whilst equipped with Havocs; on the other hand, as previously mentioned, the Twelfth Air Force later gained two additional medium bomber units when the 12th and 340th BGs were transferred from the Ninth Air Force.

Having flown its Douglas Boston IIIs—an export version of the A-20 of which a few had been obtained from Royal Air Force stock—from England, the 15th BS (Light) flew its first sorties from Tebessa, Algeria, within one week from the start of Operation *Torch.* Limited as the experience of this squadron was (only forty-eight sorties had been flown in England during a three-month period), it was none the less an asset for the Twelfth Air Force,

3. Havoc of the 647th BS, 410th BG (Light), 9th Air Force over occupied Europe, summer 1944. External 500-lb bombs may be seen on wing racks, in addition to the internal load. (USAF)

4. **Well-known veteran A-20G of the 409th BG (Light). It was named 'La France Libre' at a ceremony at Le Bourget in September 1944 when the 409th was stationed at Bretigny, near Paris. (USAF)**

as all the other light and medium bomber units had no combat experience at all; the 15th BS had flown in combat with the RAF and with the Eighth Air Force. The lack of experience was apparent as soon as groups entered combat and tried to use the low-altitude bombing techniques in which they had been trained and which had proved successful in the Pacific. However, against the more strongly defended targets in North Africa, such as airfields and harbour facilities, heavy losses were suffered whilst results were below expectations. Particularly hard hit during initial operations was the B-26-equipped 319th BG which, less than three months after flying its first mission on 28 November 1942, had to be withdrawn to Morocco for rest and re-training in medium-altitude bombing tactics. The other bombardment groups of the Twelfth Air Force, including even the 47th BG which had had many of its A-20Bs modified as strafers by mounting an additional battery of four forward-firing machine guns in place of their bombardier station, were likewise forced to bomb from altitudes of 8,000 to 14,000 ft (2,440 to 4,270 metres) in order to stay out of range of light anti-aircraft weapons. None the less, the 47th BG performed sterling services during the battle for the Kasserine Pass on 22 February 1943 when it helped stop the German offensive by flying eleven missions against armoured columns, an action for which the group was awarded a Distinguished Unit Citation.

At the time of the battle for the Kasserine Pass, when the American ground forces had their first major experience against the *Afrika Korps*, the Twelfth Air Force had only four operational twin-engined groups, the 17th and 319th BGs with B-26s, the 47th BG with A-20s, and the 310th BG with B-25s. Soon thereafter, the 320th (B-26s) and 321st (B-25s) BGs were added. On the other hand, its 68th Observation Group (made up of one Regular squadron, the 16th, and of three National Guard squadrons which had been ordered into active service—the 111th from Texas, the 122nd from Louisiana and the 154th from Arkansas) had flown its A-20Bs for only a brief period and had been re-equipped with an assortment of fighter and reconnaissance aircraft. As the Allies mounted a final offensive to oust the Axis from Africa, the light and medium bombers of the Twelfth Air Force joined fighters and heavy bombers in a massive effort to prevent the Axis from airlifting and shipping supplies and reinforcements, and to provide air support during the final phase of the African campaign. In the process, the Twelfth Air Force sank several warships and transports and destroyed a large number of German and Italian aircraft both on the ground and in the air. Not all enemy aircraft fell to the guns of the fighters as, for example, on 10 April B-25s claimed the destruction in the air of ten Junkers Ju52 transports and one Ju88 bomber whilst escorting P-38s shot down fourteen more enemy aircraft. The success of these operations contributed greatly to the defeat of the Axis forces in Tunisia which surrendered on 13 May 1943.

Immediately thereafter, the 17th, 47th, 310th, 319th, 320th and 321st BGs took part in Operation *Corkscrew*—the reduction of the strongholds of Pantelleria and Lampedusa—and in the pre-invasion air offensive against Sicily, the opening phase of Operation *Husky*. Landings on Sicily began at dawn on 10 July and for the next five weeks the light and medium bombers of the Ninth and Twelfth Air Forces, which since February 1943 were fighting under the unified command of the North African Air Force (NAAF), were constantly in action against tactical targets and airfields. On several occasions

8

their operations proved costly, such as on 11 July when a force of 36 Marauders of the 17th BG had two of its aircraft damaged beyond repair, eight badly damaged and fifteen less severely damaged whilst bombing the Trapani/Milo airfield. These operations, however, greatly assisted the hard-fighting ground forces, which by 17 August had succeeded in securing the island. The mainland of Italy was now the target.

Preceded by a series of air attacks ranging over most of Italy, the invasion of the Continent began on 3 September 1943 when British troops landed in Calabria (Operation *Baytown*) and went into full gear six days later when American and British forces landed at Salerno and Paestum, south of Naples. By then the Germans appeared to be the only enemies left as the Italians had surrendered on 8 September; however, whilst the Italian Co-

5. Formation of A-20G Havocs at typical 9th Air Force combat altitude over occupied Europe; the aircraft are from the 671st BS, 416th BG (Light). (USAF)

Belligerent forces went on to join the Allies, other Italian troops and air units in Northern Italy continued to fight alongside the Germans under the aegis of the Republica Sociale Italiana. Faced with a serious threat, the Germans stiffened their defences and brought Allied advances to a snail's pace. To support these operations three B-25 groups (the 12th, 321st and 340th BGs) and the A-20 equipped 47th BG moved to bases in Italy between 24 September and 12 November 1943 whilst during this last month the three B-26 groups (the 17th, 319th and 320th) were transferred to Sardinia. The last medium bomber unit of the Twelfth Air Force, the 310th BG, began operating from Corsica on 10 December.

6. Bomb leader A-20J of the 410th BG; while 90 per cent of the 9th AF Havocs were solid-nose A-20Gs and A-20Hs with six forward-firing 0.50 machine guns, the transparent-nose A-20Js and A-20Ks proved valuable lead bombing aircraft over frequently overcast ETO targets. (USAF)

Whereas the 47th BG flew its short-ranged A-20s mainly on tactical air support missions, the B-25 and B-26 equipped groups combined this type of mission with operations against several other types of targets. For example, in October 1943 Mitchells flew a series of strikes against airfields in Greece, Crete and Rhodes to prevent the Luftwaffe from interfering effectively against Allied operations in Southern Italy whilst Marauders concentrated their efforts on the railroad network by bombing bridges, tunnels and marshalling yards, their most famous mission of this kind taking place on 3 March 1944 when all bombs dropped by the 17th, 319th and 320th BGs fell within 200 yards of the Ostiense yard in Rome. The Twelfth Air Force's twin-engined bomber groups, less the 12th BG which was transferred to the Tenth Air Force in India at the end of January 1944, were also heavily committed to the support of the landings at Anzio and Nettuno (Operation *Shingle*) in January 1944 and the battle for Cassino. However, in spite of their efforts, the

7. This A-20J bears the black-and-white rudder stripes of the 410th BG (Light), and the white cowling bands and '7X' code of the 645th BS. Adopted in late summer 1944, these bands were red for the 644th BS, blue for the 646th and yellow for the 647th. (USAF)

Gustav Line could not be broken through by the Allied troops which took heavy casualties and were stalemated. Accordingly, the Twelfth Air Force undertook in mid-March 1944 Operation *Strangle* to disrupt the German supply network. Assisted by fighter bombers, the light and medium bombers repeatedly attacked railroads and motor transport and by mid-May had reduced daily capacity of the network from 80,000 to 4,000 tons. Deprived of the necessary supplies, the Wehrmacht was forced to retreat and Rome was taken on 4 June 1944. Air support had broken the stalemate.

Two days after the fall of Rome a new front was opened in Western Europe when the Allies landed in Normandy and, to assist operations in Northern France by preventing the Germans from bringing reinforcements from Italy, the Twelfth Air Force bombers kept on the pressure. The Twelfth also undertook the softening-up of German defences in Southern France in preparation for Operations *Anvil* and *Dragon*. On D-Day, 15 August 1944, the Marauders and Mitchells flew in direct support of the landings between Cannes and Saint Tropez and bombed road and rail bridges in the Rhône Valley and French Alps (including the Sisteron viaduct which the author saw attacked three times by B-26s but which was finally brought down by maquisards). Two days later B-25s of the 321st BG sank the battleship *Strasbourg,* the cruiser *La Gallissonière* and a submarine at Toulon, an action for which the group earned a DUC. Still based in Sardinia (B-26 groups) and Corsica (B-25 groups),

the bombers of the Twelfth Air Force continued during the autumn of 1944 to share their attention between targets in France and Italy. However, in November 1944 the 17th and 320th BGs were transferred to the First Tactical Air Force (Provisional) and moved to French bases from where they operated until VE-day in support of operations in France and Germany.

At about the same time the three B-25 groups (the 310th, 321st and 340th) were supplemented by the 319th BG which converted from B-26s to B-25s until transferred back to the United States in January 1945. The Mitchells then operated primarily against rail and road communications in Italy, Austria (notably along the Brenner Pass) and the Balkans. On shorter range missions they were supported by the 47th BG which, in the spring of 1945, was in the process of converting to Douglas A-26 Invaders and which increasingly flew its missions at night. Together these four groups inflicted considerable damage to the German transportation system and, in the closing days of the war, prevented the Wehrmacht from retreating across the Po Valley. German forces in Italy finally surrendered on 29 April 1945.

8. A-20J-10-DO, 43-9913, coded 8U-A, the Havoc of the CO, 646th BS, 410th BG was named 'Maxine IV'. Note blue cowling band and pointed flash leading back on cowling sides, and white patch over port 0.50 nose gun. (USAF)

EIGHTH AIR FORCE IN ENGLAND

Even though the primary mission assigned to the Eighth Air Force had been strategic bombing for which four-engined B-17 and B-24 heavy bombers, together with appropriate escort fighters, were to be the chosen weapons, the first sorties flown by personnel assigned to the Eighth Air Force were those made by crews of the 15th BS (Light) in twin-engined Douglas Boston IIIs during the summer of 1942. The 15th BS (L) had been activated on 11 February 1940 at Barksdale Field, Louisiana, as part of the 27th BG. After training on Curtiss A-18 and Douglas A-20A twin-engined attack bombers, this squadron was separated from its parent organization and selected for deployment to England where, under the new designation of 1st Pursuit Squadron (Night Fighter), it was to be

9. Bearing full invasion markings of five 24-in black-and-white stripes round the wings and fuselage, this A-20J-15-D0, 43-21745, 8U-S 'Irene' of the 646th BS, 410th BG (Light) was photographed at Gosfield, England, on 22 June 1944. Airscrew hubs are probably blue, though no cowling band is visible. (USAF)

trained by the RAF as the first USAAF unit to fly the Douglas Havoc (Turbinlite), a version of the Douglas light bomber fitted with a 2,700 million candle-power searchlight in the nose. On operations, however, the RAF had found the Turbinlite

10, 11. Sentimental nose art: a Mother's Day embellishment for an A-20G, and a youthful pilot posing proudly by his 'Li'l Suzie', a A-20K-I-D0 Havoc, 44-84, of the 410th BG. Note captain's bars on overseas cap and shirt collar, and pilot's wings. (USAF)

principle left much to be desired and, by May 1942 when the 1st Pursuit Squadron (Night Fighter) arrived at Grafton Underwood, Northants, the RAF had discontinued its use. Accordingly, the US unit was designated once again 15th BS (L) and was sent to Swanton Morley, Norfolk to acquire operational experience whilst flying Douglas Boston III bombers with No. 226 Squadron, RAF. On 29 June 1942 an American crew led by Capt. Charles Kegelman joined eleven crews of No. 226 Squadron in a mission against the Hazelbrouck marshalling yard in France, the first operation by USAAF personnel in the ETO. Five days later, to celebrate the American Independence Day, six US crews and six British crews flew twelve Boston IIIs of No. 226 Squadron to attack at low altitude four Luftwaffe

airfields in the Low Countries. Results were disappointing in spite of the good performance by all crews and two American- and one British-manned aircraft were lost. One more mission was flown by US crews in aircraft of the British squadron but in August 1942 the 15th BS (L) received its own Boston IIIs from RAF depots. Three missions were flown from England in aircraft bearing the US national marking until the unit was taken out of operation in early October 1942 in preparation for its movement to North Africa where it became the first operational bomber squadron of the Twelfth Air Force.

One A-20 unit, the 47th BG (L) at Horham, Suffolk; three B-26 units, the 17th BG (M) at Kimbolton, Hants, the 319th BG (M) at Horsham St Faiths, Norfolk and the 320th BG (M) at Hethel, Norfolk and the 310th BG (M) with B-25s at Hardwick, Norfolk, had been scheduled to con-

12. Formation of A-26B Invaders of the 669th BS, 416th BG (Light), 9th Air Force, photographed shortly after this unit's conversion from Havocs in November 1944. (USAF)

stitute the initial Eighth Air Force complement of twin-engined bombers. However, prior to entering combat these five groups were transferred to the Twelfth Air Force for operations in North Africa. Thus, from the time of the 15th BS (L) transfer until the spring of 1943, the Eighth Air Force did not fly combat missions with light or medium bombers. The dubious honour of flying the Eighth Air Force's first group missions with twin-engined bombers was given to the 322nd BG (Medium) which, on 14 May 1943, dispatched at low altitude twelve Martin Marauders from Bury St Edmunds, Suffolk, against a power station at Ijmuiden, Holland. One B-26 was lost and several others were damaged. The next mission against the same target and again

13. With bomb doors open, this A-26B of the 554th BS, 386th BG is seen riding a flak barrage during a mission on 20 April 1945. Originally a Marauder unit of the 8th AF, the group was re-assigned to the 9th in September 1943 and converted to Invaders early in 1945. (USAF)

at low altitude was flown three days later with catastrophic results as all eleven aircraft sent by the group failed to return. No more proof was needed to convince the 322nd BG and the Eighth Air Force that a change in tactics was called for, and the Marauders were fitted with Norden bombsights and other modifications whilst their crews began practising operations at medium altitude as used by the RAF in Northern Europe and by the Twelfth Air Force in North Africa.

Three more B-26 groups had been assigned to the Eighth Air Force and, on 16 July 1943, the 323rd BG flew the first of the medium-altitude missions to bomb the marshalling yard at Abbeville, France. In quick succession the other groups joined the 323rd BG in attacking, from medium altitude, airfields and marshalling yards, the first of these missions for

each group being flown on 17 July (386th BG), 31 July (322nd BG) and 15 August (387th BG). Usually escorted by RAF Spitfires, the Marauders of these units initially proved inaccurate in their new role. However, as experience was gained, accuracy improved greatly and, in spite of the often very intense flak, the four groups built up a good reputation. At the same time, the Marauders, which had been considered difficult aircraft to fly due to their high landing speed, began to turn in the lowest loss per sortie ratio in the Eighth Air Force. As aircraft and crews were finally proving themselves, the decision was made to transfer the four Marauder groups to provide the nucleus of the Ninth Air Force which was taking up its new assignment in the ETO. The last B-26 missions by the Eighth Air Force were flown by the 323rd and 387th BGs on 9 October 1943.

NINTH AIR FORCE OVER NORTHERN EUROPE

Beginning on 18 October 1943, when the first mission with the Ninth Air Force was flown, the four veteran B-26 groups continued their campaign against airfields and railroads in northern France and Belgium whilst they provided the necessary experience for two Combat Wings formed within the Ninth Air Force. Each of these B-26 wings was made up of two experienced groups and two new groups, the 98th CBW including the 322nd and 387th BGs as well as the 394th BG (first mission flown·on 9 March 1944) and 397th BG (20 April 1944), whilst the 99th CBW had the experienced 323rd and 368th BGs and the new 344th BG (6 March 1944) and 391st BG (25 January 1944). In addition, during February 1944 the 98th CBW added to its strength a special unit, the 1st Pathfinder Squadron (Provisional), which flew B-26s specially fitted with *Gee, Oboe* and H2X electronic equipment to enable conventionally equipped B-26s to fly night and blind bombing missions by dropping their bombs on the command of the pathfinders.

14. Although assigned to the 84th BS, 47th BG, 12th Air Force, this A-26B-20-DT carries on the nose the emblem of the 118th Tactical Reconnaissance Squadron. This Connecticut National Guard unit was at that time flying Lockheed F-5s and North American F-6s with the 23rd Fighter Group, 14th Air Force in China! (Harry Lippincott)

In early December 1943 the Marauder groups had been assigned additional targets as part of Operation *Crossbow*, the destruction of V-1 buzz bomb launching sites which were being erected in the Pas de Calais and Cherbourg areas. The first of these new missions was flown on 5 December and the V-1 launching sites became frequent targets of the Ninth Air Force until they were overrun by Allied ground forces in the late summer of 1944. Meanwhile, the Ninth Air Force bombers and fighter bombers and those of the Royal Air Force greatly impeded the German efforts and contributed substantially to limiting the number of V-1s eventually dispatched against England. In spite of the importance of Operation *Crossbow*, it was targets listed for Operation *Pointblank*—the air offensive to break the back of the Luftwaffe by bombing its airfields whilst heavy bombers concentrated their efforts on the German aircraft industry—which constituted the main objective of the Marauder groups. Their biggest contribution to Operation *Pointblank* was made on 24 and 25 February 1944 when the five B-26 groups then operational (the 322nd, 323rd, 386th, 387th and 391st BGs) made their deepest penetration so far, to bomb airfields at Deelen, Gilze Rijen, Leuwarden and Venlo, Holland, and at St Trond, Belgium.

A third wing, the 97th Combat Bombardment Wing was also formed within the Ninth Air Force and comprised the 409th, 410th and 416th BGs (Light). Equipped with solid-nosed A-20Gs and bombardier-nosed A-20Js, these groups were delayed by the need to ship their short-ranged aircraft to England and by the lack of certain types of equipment. None the less, the 461st BG went operational on 3 March 1944 and was followed on 13 April by the 409th BG and on 1 May by the 410th BG, to bring the Ninth Air Force to its full bomber complement in time for the pre-invasion offensive

15. Line of A-26Cs of the 97th BS, 47th BG at Grosetto, Italy, shortly after VE-Day. The group had just completed re-equipment with Invaders and still operated aircraft finished in both natural metal and gloss black. (USAF)

leading to the landings in Normandy on 6 June 1944. During this phase of the war, the three Combat Bombardment Wings of the Ninth Air Force bombed V-1 sites, attacked marshalling yards to disrupt enemy communications and struck at a number of coastal batteries and fortifications from the Pas de Calais to Normandy. In May 1944 road bridges were added to the list of targets to isolate Wehrmacht units, and airfields received a final going over on the eve of D-Day.

Sporting around their wings and rear fuselage the invasion stripes of five alternating white and black bands (each 20in wide on the B-26s and 24in wide on the A-20s), the eleven bombardment groups of the Ninth Air Force mounted a maximum effort on D-Day when many of their crews flew two missions. Targets during this long awaited day included coastal batteries, strong points, road junctions, bridges and marshalling yards and, even though the weather was less than ideal, the bombers created havoc in the German defences by flying 823 sorties and dropping 1,441 tons of bombs. During the following days the bombers continued to provide

effective support to the ground forces which were consolidating their hold on the Continent. They also mounted an all-out interdiction campaign against the German transportation network, thus preventing the Wehrmacht from bringing much-needed reinforcement to Normandy. None the less, the Germans succeeded in stopping the Allied advance along a line from St Lô to Caen whilst the Ninth Air Force was forced to attack again the V-1 sites as buzz bombs began to fall in England one week after the start of Operation *Torch*. The stalemate on the ground was broken on 25 July when Operation *Cobra* was unleashed and bombers and fighter bombers breached the German lines to enable Lt. Gen. George Patton's Third Army to launch its own version of 'Blitzkrieg'. Three weeks later the Ninth Air Force teamed up with the RAF during the battle to reduce the German pocket at Falaise and, under the umbrella of their black-and-white striped aircraft, the Allies rapidly advanced and soon joined up with the troops which had landed in Southern France with Twelfth Air Force support. During this period, Capt. Darrell R. Lindsey of the

394th BG was awarded posthumously the Congressional Medal of Honor for continuing to lead his formation until the bomb run, even though his B-26 was burning after being hit during an attack on 9 August 1944 against a bridge on the Seine. Capt. Lindsey remained in his aircraft to let his crew bail out and died in the ensuing crash.

In the late summer of 1944, the Ninth Air Force introduced a new and potent bomber in the ETO when the 553rd BS of the 386th BG had 18 Douglas A-26B Invaders attached to it for combat evaluation. Between 6 and 19 September these aircraft flew eight missions from the 386th BG's base at Great Dunmow, Essex, and the Ninth Air Force found the A-26 to be a very effective medium bomber with a larger load than the A-20, greater range and speed than either the A-20 or B-26, and with superior

16. A B-25 Mitchell of the 82nd BS, 12th BG, 9th AF hugs the floor of the desert on its way to the target, accompanied by six shadowy comrades! The aircraft is finished in Desert Pink and Neutral Gray, and bears the usual North African theatre marking of an RAF fin flash on inner and outer tail surfaces. (USAF)

17. The red tips to the vertical tail surfaces identify Mitchells of the 321st BG: the nearest is 43-28082, a B-25J-5-NC version, and the second is B-25D-30-NC number 43-3522. The white roman III on the tail further identifies the 447th BS. (USAF)

single-engine performance. However, due to production delays and to the need to introduce a number of modifications and improvements, the A-26 was not immediately available to re-equip a full group. Thus, having temporarily lost control of the aircraft tested by the 553rd BS, the Ninth Air Force had to wait until November 1944 to replace the A-20s of its 416th BG with A-26B Invaders and this group was forced to retain for a while its A-20J bomb leaders as no A-26C with bombardier nose was yet available. The 416th BG flew its first A-26 mission on 17 November and, two months later,

began taking advantage of the heavy forward-firing armament of its A-26Bs by flying ground-attack strafing sorties. Re-equipment of other groups proceeded at a slower pace than originally scheduled due to continued production delays. Thus, the 409th began converting to A-26s in November 1944 and became operational on the new type in early December, whilst the 386th flew A-26s beginning in February 1945 and the 391st BG followed in April 1945. A fifth group, the 410th BG, was in the midst of converting to Invaders when the war ended in Europe.

While the A-26 was making its combat debut in the ETO, the A-20s and B-26s continued to bear the brunt of operations for the 9th Bombardment Division to which the 97th, 98th and 99th Combat Bombardment Wings were reporting. The groups of

18

the 9th BD had begun moving to bases in France in August 1944 when the 323rd, 387th, 394th and 397th BGs respectively began operating from Lessay, Maupertuis, Tour-en-Bessin and Gorges, and all eleven groups were on the Continent by 2 October 1944 when the 386th arrived at Beaumont-sur-Oise. Often impaired by bad weather, the 9th Bombardment Division continued its steady campaign of interdiction and provided effective support for the ground forces which appeared poised to

18. Mitchells of the 487th BS, 340th BG, 12th Air Force display a variety of national insignia, a reminder that Technical Orders on the subject of markings were often ignored in the field. (USAF)

deliver the *coup de grâce* to the Third Reich. Fate, in the form of even worse weather and German stamina, were to foil this plan for a while longer.

On 16 December 1944, as bad weather kept most Allied aircraft on the ground, the 5th and 6th

19. Black-tailed B-25Js of the 319th BG, 9th Air Force. The 437th, 438th, 439th and 440th BSs were identified by battle numbers on the tails in the ranges 1–24, 25–49, 50–74 and 75–99 respectively. (USAF)

(SS) Panzer Armies and the 7th Army under the command of *Feldmarschall* von Rundstedt launched a powerful offensive—Operation *Greif*—against the US 1st Army in the Ardennes area. Outnumbered and deprived of their customary air support, most American troops reeled back and the Germans advanced towards Liège and threatened to cut off the British 21st Army Group. Courageously the 101st Airborne Division held its ground at Bastogne whilst the 9th Bombardment Division interfered with the German advance by joining the Eighth Air Force heavies and RAF bombers in striking at the German supply lines behind the front. Then, on 23 December, the weather began clearing up and the Ninth Air Force was again able to throw its whole weight in support of the hard pressed American

ground forces. For their part in the Battle of the Bulge, no fewer than five (the 323rd, 387th, 391st, 397th and 410th BGs) of the eleven groups of the 9th Bombardment Division were awarded Distinguished Unit Citations.

Following the battle in the Ardennes, the A-20s, A-26s and B-26s of the Ninth Air Force continued their steady rhythm of operations against road and rail networks, marshalling yards, fuel and ammunition dumps, and airfields. Then, on 3 May 1945 130 A-26s of the 386th, 391st, 409th and 416th BGs led by eight B-26s of the 1st Pathfinder Squadron bombed the Stod Ammon Plant in Czechoslovakia during the final mission of the 9th Bombardment Division. Less than six days later, at one minute after midnight on 9 May 1945, peace came back to Europe.

GROUP HISTORIES

North African and Mediterranean Theatres of Operations

12TH BOMBARDMENT GROUP (MEDIUM)

The first full medium or light bombardment group to be used by the USAAF in the war against Germany was 12th BG which had been assigned for service with the United States Army Middle East Air

20. Proudly displaying 68 white bombs on a black background, this veteran B-25J-1-NC bears yellow markings trimmed with black. The wide top band identifies the 310th BG and the narrow bottom band the 381st BS. The lower band changed colour with the squadron: white for the 379th BS, light blue for the 380th and red for the 428th. (USAF)

Force (USAMEAF). On 15 January 1941 this group had been activated at McChord Field, Washington, as a light bomber group and then flew a variety of aircraft. However, by the end of 1941 it had become a B-25 medium bomber unit. During July/August 1942 the 12th BG (M) flew its B-25Cs across the South Atlantic and Africa to Deversoir, Egypt, from where the first combat sorties were flown on the night of 16 August. Still flying Mitchells and assigned to the Ninth Air Force, the group was successively moved forward to bases in Libya, Tunisia and Sicily where, on 22 August 1943, it was transferred to the Twelfth Air Force. By early November 1943 the 12th BG (M) was operating on the Italian mainland but its days in the MTO were numbered as on 30 January 1944 it was re-assigned to the Tenth Air Force in India for operations against the Japanese.

Whilst operating in the Western Desert and Sicily with the Ninth Air Force the group had earned a DUC. It was composed of the 81st, 82nd, 83rd and 434th Bombardment Squadrons and the B-25s of these squadrons respectively bore on the outside of their tail surfaces battle numbers in the 1 to 25, 26 to 50, 51 to 75 and 76 to 99 ranges.

21. Mitchells of the 340th BG were identified by a letter/number combination on the outer tail surfaces. The number was the last digit of the squadron number (i.e., 6 for the 486th BS, 7 for the 487th, 8 for the 488th, 9 for the 489th) and the letter was the individual aircraft identification. (USAF)

17TH BOMBARDMENT GROUP (MEDIUM)

Flying Martin Marauders with the Twelfth Air Force until transferred to the First Tactical Air Force (Provisional) on 15 November 1944, the 17th BG (M) had been activated ten years before the war (15 July 1931) as the 17th Pursuit Group. In 1935 it had been redesignated an Attack Group and, in 1939, had become a Bombardment Group. During the later part of the summer of 1941 it had become the first unit to fly the new North American Mitchell but, within a year, it had been re-equipped with Martin Marauders. After ferrying its B-26Bs via the North Atlantic and England, the 17th BG (M) began combat operations on 30 December 1942 whilst assigned to the Twelfth Air Force. At that time the unit was based at Telergma, Algeria, and for its first mission it bombed the Gabes aerodrome.

After taking part in the operations in North Africa, the 17th BG assisted in the reduction of the Italian bases on Pantelleria and Lampedusa prior to shifting its operations to Sicily in support of the Allied landings in July 1943. Stationed in Tunisia since June 1943, the group also bombed targets on the Italian mainland, and missions against targets in Southern Europe—including support for the landings at Anzio and Nettuno in January 1944 and in southern France in August 1944—continued from Sardinia where the group had been transferred in November 1943. A first DUC was awarded to the 17th BG during that period for its role in bombing airfields around Rome on 13 January 1944. The unit moved to Corsica in September 1944 and then to Dijon, France, where on 15 November 1944 it was re-assigned to the First Tactical Air Force (Pro-

22

visional) to support Allied operations in eastern France and Germany. In the process the group earned another DUC for bombing attacks against enemy defences at Schweinfurt on 10 April 1945.

Until July 1943 the Marauders of the 17th BG did not carry unit markings. Afterwards a red band was painted around the rear fuselage just ahead of the tail gunner's position, and battle numbers in the 1 to 24, 25 to 49, 50 to 74 and 75 to 99 ranges were painted on the vertical tail surfaces of the aircraft of the 34th, 37th, 95th and 432nd Bombardment Squadrons respectively.

47TH BOMBARDMENT GROUP (LIGHT)

This unit was the only bombardment group to operate exclusively Douglas attack bombers, A-20 Havocs and A-26 Invaders, in the North African and Mediterranean theatres of operations. The group had been activated at McChord Field, Washington on 15 January 1941 and, after flying anti-submarine patrols along the West Coast, it had been trained for assignment overseas. It ferried its aircraft over the North Atlantic in October 1942 and, after a few weeks in England, flew them to North Africa to join the Twelfth Air Force. Combat operations with A-20B-DLs began on 16 December 1942 from Youks-les-Bains, Algeria, and the 47th BG (L) quickly specialized in low-level interdiction and ground-support operations. These missions were carried out with increasing effectiveness and, during the battle for the Kasserine Pass in February 1943, the 47th BG (L) won a DUC for its role in helping to stop the German offensive in this important sector. Following the progress of Allied ground troops, the 47th BG (L) moved to bases in Tunisia (from 30 March 1943), Malta (from 21 July), Sicily (from 9 August) and Italy (from 24 September). With the exception of a two-month period in the summer of 1944, when it operated from Corsica and southern France in support of Operation *Anvil* and the subsequent advance up the Rhône valley, the group remained in Italy until VE-Day. During the last ten months of the war the 47th BG (L) added night interdiction sorties to its repertoire, and a combination of day and night sorties flown from 21 to 24 April 1945, which succeeded in disrupting the German retreat in the

22. Bombs away! B-26B-40-MA, 42-43291, of the 439th BS, 319th BG, 12th Air Force, unloads four 1,000-lb bombs. (NA&SM).

Po valley, earned a second DUC for the group.

Battle numbers were applied on the fin and rudder of the 47th's A-20s and on the fin of A-26s— the Invaders supplementing the Havocs from January/February 1945—and the ranges 1 to 24, 25 to 49, 50 to 74 and 75 to 99 identified aircraft from the 84th, 85th, 86th and 97th Squadrons respectively.

310TH BOMBARDMENT GROUP (MEDIUM)

Activated on 15 March 1942 as one of the first wartime groups, the 310th BG (M) was trained in the southern United States until 24 September when it began ferrying its B-25Cs across the North Atlantic to England. Deployment to Morocco and Algeria began shortly after the onset of Operation *Torch* and the group flew its first mission, a bombing raid against the harbour at Sousse, Tunisia on 2 December 1942. The Mitchells of the 310th BG (M) were active throughout the North African campaign

and went on to bomb targets on Pantelleria and Lampedusa and in Sicily and Italy from bases in Algeria and Tunisia. Operating from Temime, Tunisia, the group won a DUC on 27 August 1943 for its effective bombing of the Benevento marshalling yard in Italy in spite of intense attacks by enemy fighters (three B-25s were lost but the 310th claimed the destruction of eighteen enemy aircraft). The 310th BG (M) was transferred to Corsica on 10 December 1943 and operated from this island until it moved to Fano, Italy in the last month of the war. Whilst based in Corsica, the group continued operating against the German communication network in Italy—with occasional missions to Yugoslavia and Austria—and supported the invasion of southern France in August 1944. A second DUC was won by the 310th BG (M) on 10 March 1945

23, 24. Photographed after her return to the USA in September 1943, 'Lady Halitosis' was a 43-mission veteran of the 17th BG, 12th Air Force. The B-26B-MA Marauder, 41-17765, was commanded by Lt. William van Marter, who is first on the left in the close-up. (USAF)

during an attack against the railroad bridge at Ora.

Group markings in the form of a yellow horizontal band around the vertical tail surfaces of its Mitchells were first applied by the 310th BG (M) in the middle of 1943. Six months later a narrower band was applied below the group band to identify the component squadrons, the colour of this band being white on aircraft of the 379th BS, light blue for those of the 380th BS, yellow for those of the 381st BS, and red on those of the 428th BS.

319TH BOMBARDMENT GROUP (MEDIUM)

Equipped with B-26Bs, this unit had been activated at Barksdale Field, Louisiana on 19 June 1942 and had begun its deployment overseas less than four months later by ferrying its aircraft over the North Atlantic to Horsham St Faith in England. During the

Captain pilot, US 9th Air Force, 1944. This officer wears one of the optional uniform combinations: olive service tunic with olive peaked cap and 'pink' trousers. The characteristically battered 'fifty mission cap' has brown leather peak and strap and gilt national insignia. The tunic collar bears the 'U.S.' cypher on each upper lapel and the Air Force's winged propeller badge on each lower lapel. Pilot's wings are worn in silver on the left breast, above gallantry and campaign ribbons. Captain's rank bars appear on the tunic shoulder-straps, and the line of dark wool braid round each cuff indicates commissioned rank. The 9th Air Force patch is sewn to the left shoulder only.

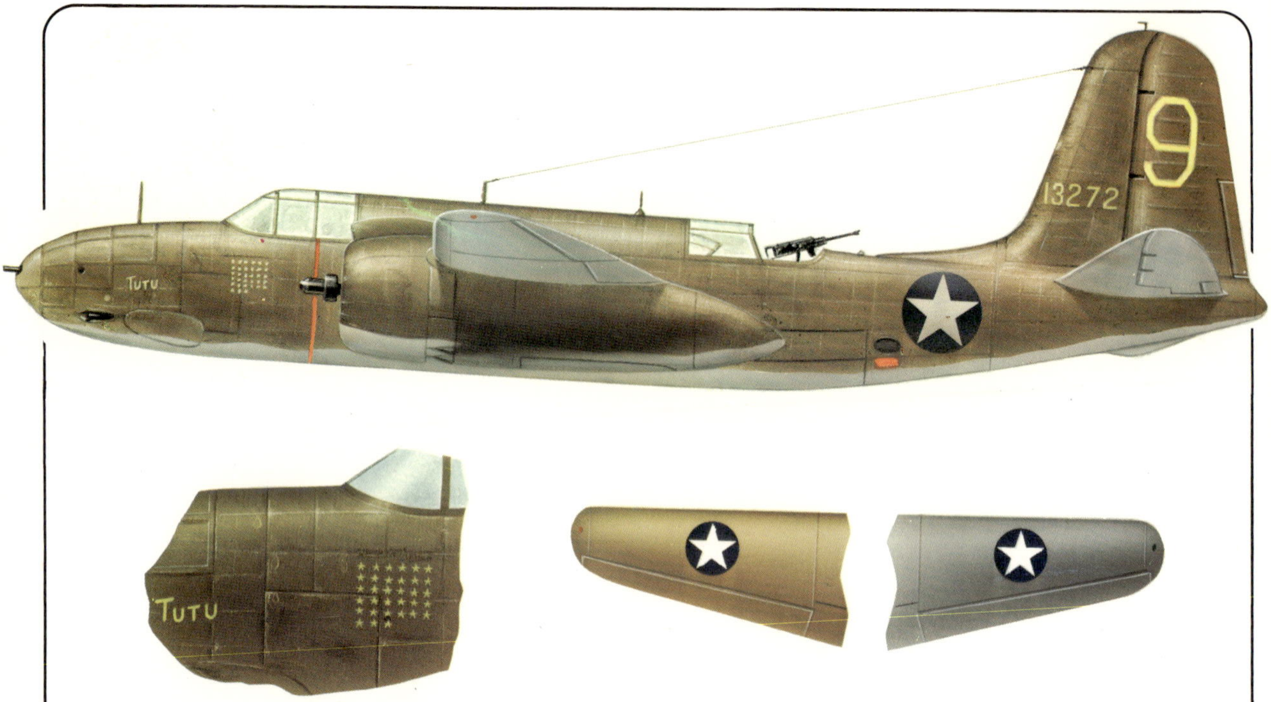

DOUGLAS A-20B-DL HAVOC, 41-3272, of 84th Bomb Sqn, 47th Bomb Gp (Light), 12th Air Force; May 1943

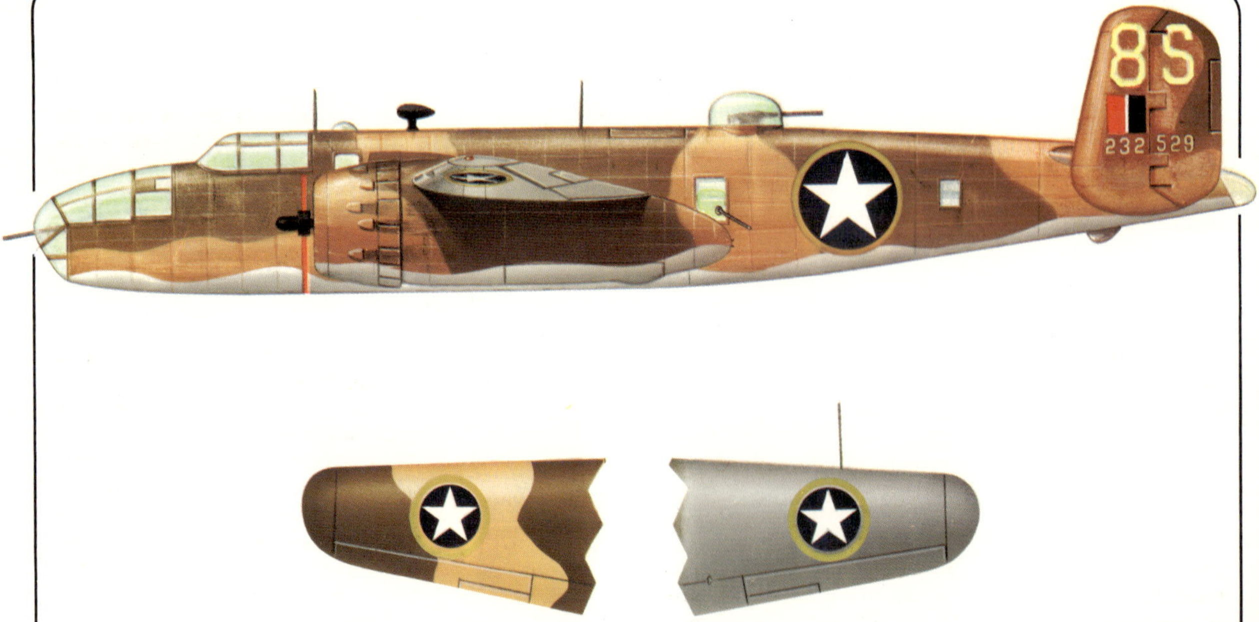

NORTH AMERICAN B-25C-15-NA MITCHELL, 42-32529, of 488th Bomb Sqn, 340th Bomb Gp (Medium), 9th Air Force; May 1943

DOUGLAS A-20K-15-DO HAVOC, 44-613, of 645th Bomb Sqn, 410th Bomb Gp (Light), 9th Air Force; February 1945

OPPOSITE, TOP: Douglas A-20B-DL Havoc of the 84th Bombardment Squadron, 47th Bombardment Group (Light), 12th Air Force, as it appeared at Souk-el-Arba, Tunisia, in May 1943. The aircraft is finished in Olive Drab and Neutral Gray, with a red propeller warning stripe round the fuselage. Note the painted-over nose transparency; the aircraft had been fitted with extra nose guns in the field. There are no unit markings as such; the yellow '9' on the tail is the individual aircraft's 'battle number'. The last five letters of the serial number, (4)1-3272, are painted on each side of the tail. The name 'Tutu' and the mission tally of yellow stars have been added by the crew. Patch views show nose markings and national insignia positions on top of port and below starboard wings.

OPPOSITE, BOTTOM: North American B-25C-15-NA Mitchell of the 488th Bombardment Squadron, 340th Bombardment Group (Medium), 9th Air Force, based at Sfax, Tunisia, in May 1943. In contrast to the previous plate, this aircraft is distinctly British-looking. The original Desert Pink and Neutral Gray scheme has had shadow camouflage added in Olive Drab; and, to avoid confusion in a theatre long dominated by the RAF, the

fin flash of that service is painted on both sides of the vertical tail surfaces. The tail marking '8S' identifies the aircraft ('S') and the squadron, '8' being the last digit of the squadron number. The radio call number is, conventionally, the last six digits of the serial (4)2-32529. The national insignia have a six-inch yellow surround. Once again, the patch views illustrate the asymmetrical wing insignia.

ABOVE: Douglas A-20K-15-DO Havoc of the 645th Bombardment Squadron, 410th Bombardment Group (Light), 9th Air Force, based at Juvincourt, France, in February 1945. The aircraft is finished in glossy black overall (shade Jet ANA 622) but has been fitted with a replacement rudder finished in a shadow camouflage of Olive Drab and Medium Green. The squadron is identified by the code '7X', and by the white cowling ring; the individual aircraft, by the code 'T' and the radio call-sign number in dull red on the tail—this takes the usual form (4)4-613. Note the light grey wash over the fuselage and wing insignia; and the name 'Helen' in red letters trimmed with yellow on the nose. There is extensive weathering on the engine nacelles and wings.

27

MARTIN B-26B-45-MA MARAUDER, 42-95793, of 444th Bomb Sqn, 320th Bomb Gp (Medium), 1st Allied Tactical Air Force; spring 1945

PAGES 28–29: Martin B-26B-45-MA Marauder of the 444th Bombardment Squadron, 320th Bombardment Group (Medium), 1st Allied Tactical Air Force, based at Dijon/Longvic, France, in the spring of 1945. This conventionally finished Marauder in Olive Drab and Neutral Gray warpaint is enlivened by the eyes and mouth of the shark suggested by the shape of the fuselage; this shark-mouth was a squadron motif. The 10-inch yellow band beneath the tailplane, around the rear fuselage, is a group identification, and the yellow battle number on the fin and rudder identifies the individual aircraft. The six-digit radio call-sign is conventional, as are the national insignia. The wing markings have 40-inch diameter discs with a two-inch blue surround to the bars; the fuselage discs are 30 inches in diameter and have 1½-inch blue surrounds to the bars.

BELOW: Douglas A-26C-25-DT Invader, 43-22641, of the 574th Bombardment Squadron, 391st Bombardment Group (Medium), 9th Air Force, based at Assche, Belgium, in April 1945. At this late stage of the war in Europe, Germany's day fighter force was virtually eliminated through lack of fuel and safe airfields, and camouflage shades had generally given way to natural metal finish as the value of obscurity disappeared. The black code '4L' identifies the squadron, 'V' the individual aircraft, and the yellow and black tail triangle, the group.

OPPOSITE, TOP: Individual emblems. (1) is that carried by a B-25C Mitchell of the 83rd Bombardment Squadron, 12th Bombardment Group at Medenine, Tunisia, in the spring of 1943. The fin markings are shown on the right. The aircraft was finished Olive Drab/Neutral Gray, and bore no other markings apart from the conventional national insignia of a white star on a blue disc in four positions. (2) is the nose marking of a B-26B-25 Marauder of the 554th Bombardment Squadron, 386th Bombardment Group, 9th Air Force, based at Boxted, England, in 1943–44. The Marauder was painted Olive Drab/Neutral Gray overall, with the radio call-sign 131877 in yellow on the fin and rudder beneath a broad yellow horizontal band. Dull red codes RU-V were painted on the fuselage, and conventional star-and-bar national insignia appeared in four positions. (3) is the port nose emblem of a B-25C-5 Mitchell, 42-53451, of an unknown unit. The tail marking illustrated on the right is the only other marking in the photograph from which this insignia was illustrated, apart from yellow-bordered star-on-disc national insignia. (4) is the starboard nose presentation of the same Mitchell's emblem—note differences. This view was taken from a second photograph, obviously of different date, in which the yellow bar had disappeared from the tail surfaces and the yellow surround from the national insignia.

OPPOSITE, BELOW: Open-cab version of the Model 969A Wrecker Truck on the basic 4-ton 6 × 6 Diamond T truck chassis. This heavy crane was used on USAAF airfields for emergency work, such as lifting crashed aircraft.

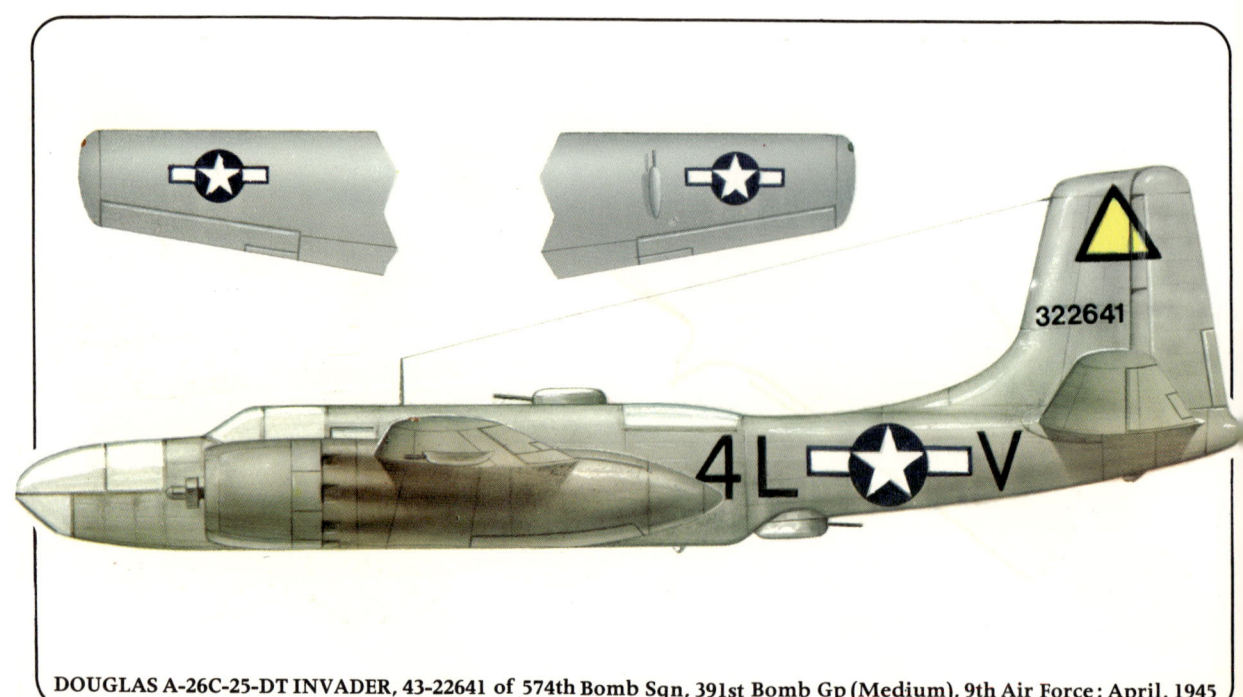

DOUGLAS A-26C-25-DT INVADER, 43-22641 of 574th Bomb Sqn, 391st Bomb Gp (Medium), 9th Air Force; April, 1945

1

2

3

253 451

4

4-ton, 6 × 6 Diamond T Model 969A Wrecker Truck

Lieutenant, US 9th Air Force, 1944. This aircrew officer, a pilot or navigator, wears the sort of casual dress commonly seen around operational airfields in Europe. The olive overseas cap is piped with gold and black cord and bears the rank bar pinned to the left side. This is repeated on the shoulder-straps of the brown leather jacket, which has a zip front and olive knitted waist-band and cuffs. A 9th Air Force patch is worn on the left shoulder, and a nickname is painted on the chest. The trousers are those of the Olive Drab wool service uniform, and the boots are regulation A-6 type.

Technical Sergeant, US 12th Air Force, Mediterranean theatre of operations, 1943–44. This aircrew NCO wears the wings of his speciality on the left breast, and the chevrons and 'rocker' of his rank in black on both sleeves. The light tropical and summer shirtsleeve uniform—'chinos'—is worn here as smart walking-out dress, with a tie tucked into the shirt and a narrow web belt with a plain brass buckle-plate. The sidecap is in the same light material, and is piped round the turn-up with mixed orange and ultramarine cord, the colours of the Army Air Force. The shoulder patch, on the left sleeve only, is that of the Air Force in general rather than one of the specific commands.

following month the 319th BG (M) flew its aircraft across France to begin operations from Maison Blanche, Algeria on 28 November (its first aircraft had landed at St Leu, Algeria, twenty days earlier on the first day of Operation *Torch*). After a period of very intensive operations from Algerian bases, the group was sent back to Morocco for rest and re-organization in the spring of 1943. Operations were resumed in June of that year when the 319th BG (M) joined the other units taking part in the reduction of Pantelleria and Lampedusa and supporting landings in Sicily and southern Italy. In November 1943 the unit moved to Sardinia to carry out interdictory operations in central Italy and to support ground forces during the battles for Anzio, Cassino and Rome. Two DUCs were won by the 319th BG (M) during the month of March 1944 for missions against rail facilities in Rome on the 3rd and in Florence on the 11th. Six months later the group advanced to Corsica where it was re-equipped with B-25s in November 1944. However, in January 1945 the group was withdrawn from the MTO and returned to the United States for training on A-26s and re-assignment to the Seventh Air Force in the Pacific.

Unit markings applied to the 319th Group's Marauders and Mitchells consisted of battle numbers (respectively 1 to 24, 25 to 49, 50 to 74 and 75 to 99 for aircraft of its 437th, 438th, 439th and 440th Squadrons) painted on the vertical tail surfaces (outboard only on the twin-tailed B-25s). In addition, a white band was painted around the rear fuselage of its Marauders.

320TH BOMBARDMENT GROUP (MEDIUM)
The third and last B-26 group of the Twelfth Air Force was activated at MacDill Field, Florida on 23 June 1942 and ferried its aircraft across the South Atlantic route. It entered combat operations from Montesquieu, Algeria on 22 April 1943, three weeks before the Axis forces in Africa surrendered. From then on, most of the group's activities were directed against airfields and communications on Pantelleria, in Sardinia, Sicily and Italy, or were in support of Allied ground forces, notably during the landings at Salerno, Anzio, Nettuno and southern France and the battles for Naples, Cassino, the Volturno River and Rome. These operations were conducted from bases in Tunisia and, from November 1943, in Sardinia. The 320th BG (M) then operated from Corsican bases between 18 September and 11 November 1944 in support of American and French troops moving up the Rhône valley. The group's affiliation with these forces was further strengthened on 15 November when it was transferred to the First Tactical Air Force (Provisional) for operations from bases in France.

The 320th BG (M) earned two DUCs, one resulting from the bombing of troop concentrations at Fondi, Italy, on 12 May 1944 and the other for the destruction of fortifications within the Siegfried Line on 15 March 1945.

Upon commencing operations in Algeria the group's aircraft had been identified by single individual letters painted on the rear fuselage ahead of the insignia. However, from July 1943 its Marauders used the same system of unit markings as applied to B-26s of the 17th and 319th BGs; these consisted of a yellow band around the rear fuselage just ahead of the tail gunner's position, designating the 320th BG, and battle numbers on the vertical tail surfaces (the 441st, 442nd, 443rd and 444th BS using numbers between 1 and 24, 25 and 49, 50 and 74, and 75 and 99 respectively).

321ST BOMBARDMENT GROUP (MEDIUM)
After ferrying its B-25Cs over the South Atlantic route, the 321st BG (M) began operations on 15 March 1943 from Ain M'lila, Algeria. The group, which had been activated at Barksdale Field, Louisiana on 26 June 1942, immediately distinguished itself by sinking 7 ships, probably sinking 14 more and damaging 29 other vessels during its first two weeks in combat. Whilst operating from Tunisian bases the 321st continued its offensive against enemy shipping, supported the landings in Sicily and Italy, and began operating a number of B-25Gs fitted with a forward-firing 75mm cannon (first use in the MTO of this new weapon was made on 5 August 1943 during an attack against the Guspini railway switching station in Sardinia). On 3 October 1943 the group moved to Grottaglie, Italy,

from where five days later it flew a mission against an aerodrome outside Athens, for which it was awarded its first DUC.

Missions against targets in Italy and the Balkans continued to be flown from Italian bases until 23 April 1944 when the 321st BG (M) was transferred to Corsica for operations over northern Italy and southern France. A second DUC was won by the group on 18 August 1944 when it bombed French warships in Toulon harbour to prevent their use by the Germans. The group remained in Corsica until 1 April 1945 and then moved to Gaudo, Italy, where it was based when, on 29 April, German forces in Italy surrendered.

The 321st BG (M) first painted the tips of its B-25's tails red during the summer of 1943 and in early 1944 added a white roman numeral on the outer tail

25, 26. Another much-inscribed Marauder, B-26B-2-MA, 41-17903, 'Hell Cat' of the 34th BS, 17th BG. The group posing in the close-up are the crews of 'Lady Halitosis', 'Hell Cat', and a third veteran Marauder, 'Jabbo the Sky King II'. Back row, second left, is Capt. Henry A. Potter, who was Maj. Gen. James H. Doolittle's navigator on the famous Tokyo raid of April 1942. (USAF)

surfaces to identify the squadron to which the aircraft belonged (I for the 445th, II for the 446th, III for the 447th, and IV for the 448th BS). In January 1945 these roman numerals were replaced by individual arabic battle numbers in the 1 to 25, 26 to 50, 51 to 75, and 76 to 99 ranges.

340TH BOMBARDMENT GROUP (MEDIUM)

Joining the Ninth Air Force as the battle in the Western Desert was entering its final phase, this group had been activated at the Columbia Army Air Base, South Carolina, on 20 August 1942 and had flown its B-25s over the South Atlantic and across Africa. After flying some sorties with the 12th BG (M) from El Assa, the 340th BG (M) flew its first group mission from Sfax, Tunisia, on 19 April 1943. Whilst assigned to the Ninth Air Force the group supported operations in Tunisia and Sicily and was awarded a DUC for its sustained efforts during the April–August 1943 period. However, on 22 August 1943 the 340th BG (M) was transferred to the Twelfth Air Force with which it flew interdiction and support missions from bases in Sicily (August through October 1943) and Italy (October 1943

through April 1944). The group moved to Corsica on 14 April 1944 and operated from this island until the last month of the war, when it returned to Italy to be based at Rimini. A second DUC was awarded to the 340th BG (M) for the sinking of the cruiser *Taranto* at La Spezia on 22 September 1944, thus preventing the Germans from scuttling this warship to block the entrance of this important harbour.

Whilst assigned to the Ninth Air Force, the 340th BG (M) had adopted a unique type of identification marking which was painted on the outer tail surfaces of its Mitchells. This consisted of a number and a letter, the number being the last digit of the squadron number (i.e., 6 for the 486th, 7 for the 487th, 8 for the 488th and 9 for the 489th) whereas the letter identified individual aircraft within each squadron. This type of marking continued to be used after the transfer of the 340th BG (M) to the Twelfth Air Force.

European Theatre of Operations

322ND BOMBARDMENT GROUP (MEDIUM)

The first Marauder-equipped Bombardment Group (Medium) to enter combat in the ETO with the Eighth Air Force was the 322nd which had been activated at MacDill Field, Florida, on 19 June 1942. The group's ground echelon had arrived in the United Kingdom at the end of November 1942, but its first aircraft, ferried via the South Atlantic and North Africa to avoid the bad weather over the North Atlantic ferry route, did not arrive in England until March 1943. Trained in low-altitude bombing, the 322nd BG (M) flew its first mission on 14 May 1943 when it bombed an electrical generating plant near Ijmuiden on the Dutch coast. A repeat attack against the same target three days later ended in disaster. Thirty-two medium-altitude missions were then flown by the group until 16 October

SPECIFICATIONS	A-20G-10-DO	A-26B-15-DL	B-25C-10-NA	B-25J-15-NC	B-26B-2-MA	B-26G-5-MA
DIMENSIONS:						
Span, ft in	61 4	70 0	67 7	67 7	65 0	71 0
(m)	(18.69)	(21.34)	(20.60)	(20.60)	(19.81)	(21.64)
Length, ft in	48 0	50 0	52 11	52 11	58 3	56 1
(m)	(14.63)	(15.24)	(16.13)	(16.13)	(17.75)	(17.09)
Height, ft in	17 7	18 6	15 9	15 9	19 10	20 4
(m)	(5.36)	(5.64)	(4.80)	(4.80)	(6.05)	(6.20)
Wing area, sq ft	464	540	610	610	602	658
(sq m)	(43.107)	(50.168)	(56.671)	(56.671)	(55.928)	(61.130)
WEIGHTS:						
Empty weight, lb	15,984	22,370	20,300	19,480	22,380	23,700
(kg)	(7,250)	(10,147)	(9,208)	(8,836)	(10,151)	(10,750)
Loaded weight, lb	16,870	27,600	26,122	26,122	27,200	31,600
(kg)	(7,652)	(12,519)	(11,849)	(11,849)	(12,338)	(14,334)
Maximum weight, lb	27,200	35,000	34,000	35,000	34,000	38,000
(kg)	(12,338)	(15,876)	(15,422)	(15,876)	(15,422)	(17,237)
Wing loading, lb/sq ft	36.4	51.1	42.8	42.8	45.2	48.1
(kg/sq m)	(177.5)	(249.5)	(209.1)	(209.1)	(220.6)	(234.5)
Power loading, lb/hp	5.3	6.9	7.7	7.7	6.8	7.9
(kg/hp)	(2.4)	(3.1)	(3.5)	(3.5)	(3.1)	(3.6)
PERFORMANCE:						
Maximum speed, mph @ ft	339 @ 12,400	355 @ 15,000	284 @ 15,000	275 @ 13,000	317 @ 14,500	277 @ 10,000
(km/h @ m)	(545 @ 3,780)	(571 @ 4,570)	(457 @ 4,570)	(442 @ 3,960)	(510 @ 4,420)	(446 @ 3,050)
Cruising speed, mph @ ft	272 @ 10,000	284 @ 15,000	237 @ 10,000	204 @ 10,000	260 @ 10,000	225 @ 10,000
(km/h @ m)	(438 @ 3,050)	(457 @ 4,570)	(381 @ 3,050)	(328 @ 3,050)	(418 @ 3,050)	(362 @ 3,050)
Climb rate, ft/min	10,000/7.1	10,000/8.1	15,000/16.5	15,000/19.0	15,000/12.0	15,000/24.5
(m/min)	(3,050/7.1)	(3,050/8.1)	(4,570/16.5)	(4,570/19.0)	(4,570/12.0)	(4,570/24.5)
Service ceiling, ft	25,800	22,100	21,200	24,200	23,500	20,000
(m)	(7,865)	(6,735)	(6,460)	(7,375)	(7,165)	(6,095)
Normal range, miles	1,090	1,400	1,500	1,350	1,150	1,300
(km)	(1,755)	(2,255)	(2,415)	(2,170)	(1,850)	(2,090)
Maximum range, miles	2,100	3,200	2,750	2,700	2,800	2,100
(km)	(3,380)	(5,150)	(4,425)	(4,345)	(4,505)	(3,380)

1943, when it was re-assigned to the Ninth Air Force.

Following its transfer to the Ninth Air Force, the 322nd BG (M) continued to attack airfields, marshalling yards and industrial targets in occupied Europe and, in the process, helped to prove the effectiveness of the medium bombers. For this role the group was awarded a DUC. In the spring of 1944 the 322nd BG (M) began operating more frequently against tactical targets such as bridges, fuel and ammunition dumps and V-1 launching sites, and on D-Day it bombed gun batteries and coastal defences

27. Returning from an Italian mission, Marauders of the 319th BG's 437th and 440th Bombardment Squadrons fly over the Mediterranean in close formation. (USAF)

in Normandy. Tactical air operations continued until VE-Day, the group moving to the Continent in September 1944 to operate from Beauvais/Tille, France, and Le Culot, Belgium. Whilst operating with the Eighth Air Force, the 322nd BG (M) had applied squadron codes and individual aircraft letters on the fuselage sides of its Marauders. Aircraft of its 449th through 451st Squadrons were identified respectively by the codes PN, ER, SS and DR. No other type of unit markings were used by the group.

323RD BOMBARDMENT GROUP (MEDIUM)

Activated at the Columbia Army Air Base, South Carolina on 4 August 1942, the 323rd BG (M) began operating as part of the 3rd Bombardment Wing of the Eighth Air Force on 16 July 1943. Based at Earls Colne, Essex, the group shared the same types of medium-altitude bombing missions as flown by the

322nd and was also transferred to the Ninth Air Force during October 1943. The 323rd BG (M) distinguished itself during the week of 20–25 February 1944, when the USAAF struck a series of telling blows to the Luftwaffe by bombing airfields and aircraft manufacturing plants. Interdiction and ground-support missions became the group's basic types of operation in May 1944 and, beginning in August of that year, some of these missions were flown at night. The group had moved to Beaulieu, England on 21 July 1944 but, from the 26th of August until VE-Day it operated from airfields in France (Lessay, Chartres, Laon/Athies, and Denain/Prouvy). Whilst operating from Laon/Athies the 323rd BG (M) contributed to

28. Last seconds of a doomed Marauder hit by flak during a mission to Toulon harbour. The shot-away starboard engine is still turning its four-blade airscrew, as blazing fuel erupts from the tanks in the wing. The aircraft crashed into the city. (USAF)

March 1944 to VE-Day). Whilst operational the group flew from Stansted, England until 30 September 1944 when it was moved to Cormeilles-en-Vexin, France; it then spent the last four weeks of the war at Florennes/Juzaine in Belgium from where its last wartime mission was flown on 25 April 1945. The only DUC won by the 344th BG (M) and its 494th through 497th BSs (with aircraft respectively coded K9, Y5, N3 and 7I) was awarded for missions against troop concentrations, supply dumps and bridges, flown between 24 and 26 July 1944 in support of ground operations in the St Lô area of Normandy. Group marking was a white triangle—with black outline only on natural metal finish aircraft—painted on the tail of the Marauders.

386TH BOMBARDMENT GROUP (MEDIUM)
In spite of being on operations since 30 July 1943 when it flew its first mission with the Eighth Air Force from Boxted, Essex, the 386th BG (M) was the only Marauder group in the ETO which did not receive a DUC. None the less, the group had a distinguished combat history during which it bombed airfields, transportation facilities, V-1 sites and industrial targets and provided support for ground forces during the landing in Normandy, the battle for the Falaise gap, the Ardennes campaign and the crossing of the Rhine. The 386th BG (M) had been activated at MacDill Field, Florida, on 1 December 1942. After commencing to fly combat operations from Boxted, the group moved to Great Dunmow on 24 September 1943 and, three weeks later, was transferred from the Eighth to the Ninth Air Force.

Whilst based at Great Dunmow its 553rd BS flew eight missions to test the new Douglas A-26B Invader under ETO combat conditions. However, following this experiment which took place in September 1944, the group and its 552nd through 555th Squadrons (with aircraft respectively coded RG, AN, RU and YA) continued to fly B-26 Marauders until February 1945 when it fully converted to A-26 Invaders.

In addition to its squadron codes, the 386th BG (M) was identified by a yellow horizontal band painted around the vertical tail surfaces of its B-26s

halting the German offensive in the Ardennes by repeatedly hitting the Wehrmacht transportation system, and was awarded a DUC.

Squadron codes (VT for the 453rd, RJ for the 454th, YU for the 455th, WT for the 456th BS) and individual aircraft letters were applied on the fuselage sides of the group's Marauders when it was serving with the Eighth Air Force. When the 323rd BG (M) joined the Ninth Air Force these markings were supplemented by a white band painted horizontally around the upper vertical tail surfaces of its aircraft.

344TH BOMBARDMENT GROUP (MEDIUM)
Activated at MacDill Field, Florida, on 8 September 1942, the 344th BG (M) flew Marauders in combat with the Ninth Air Force for fourteen months (6

and A-26s. On natural metal finish aircraft this band was outlined in black.

387TH BOMBARDMENT GROUP (MEDIUM)
Fourth and last Marauder group to join the Eighth Air Force, the 387th BG (M) flew twenty-nine missions between 15 August and 9 October 1943 prior to being transferred to the Ninth Air Force. Like the 386th BG (M), it had been activated at MacDill Field, Florida, on 1 December 1942. It operated from Chipping Ongar, Essex until 18 July 1944 when it moved to Stony Cross; five weeks later the group transferred to France to be stationed successively at Mauperthuis, Châteaudun and Clastres. Equipped with B-26s until the end of the war, the four squadrons (556th through 559th BS) of the group used the codes FW, KS, KX and TQ when it began operations with the Eighth Air Force but, upon joining the Ninth Air Force, a group marking consisting of a black and yellow, diagonally-striped horizontal band was painted around the vertical tail surfaces of its aircraft.

The 387th BG (M) was amongst the Ninth Air Force units which bore the brunt of air operations during the Battle of the Bulge and it was awarded a DUC for hitting strongly-defended transportation and communication targets during this critical phase of the war.

391ST BOMBARDMENT GROUP (MEDIUM)
Flying Marauders and, from April 1945, Invaders with a yellow triangle (outlined in black on natural metal finish aircraft) on their vertical tail surfaces, the 572nd through 575th Bombardment Squadrons of the 391st BG (M) were assigned the codes P2, T6, 4L and O8 respectively.

The group had been activated at MacDill Field, Florida on 21 January 1943. After moving to England at the beginning of 1944, it entered operations on 15 February from Matching, Essex. On 19 September 1944 the unit moved to Roye/Amy, France, where it remained until replaced at Assche, Belgium, on 16 April 1945.

In common with other B-26 groups of the Ninth Air Force, the 391st BG (M) was initially involved in bombing operations against airfields, V-1 sites,

29. Details of bomb bay and gun positions may be seen in this photograph of a Marauder of the 319th BG about to bomb a rail bridge at Incisa, Italy. (NA&SM)

marshalling yards and bridges. Later the group supported ground operations in France, notably during the breakthrough at St Lô, and concentrated its attacks on the German transportation system. During the Battle of the Bulge, when it operated without fighter escort in the face of intense flak and determined enemy aircraft opposition, the 391st BG (M) was one of the five bomb groups of the Ninth Air Force to be awarded a DUC.

394TH BOMBARDMENT GROUP (MEDIUM)
Entering combat on 23 March 1944 from its base at Boreham, England, the 394th BG (M) had been trained in Oklahoma and Michigan after being activated at MacDill Field, Florida, on 5 March 1943. Within less than five months from its operational debut the group had its moment of glory when, during a three-day period (7 through 9 August 1944), it bombed fortified targets and ammunition dumps and put out of action four bridges to win a

DUC whilst Capt. Darrell Lindsey was awarded a posthumous Congressional Medal of Honor.

During 1944 the 394th BG (M) was successively relocated to Holmsley, Hants, and to bases in France (Bricy, from 18 September, and Cambrai/Niergnies from 8 October). On 20 April 1945 the group flew its final mission and, less than two weeks later, moved to Venlo, Holland, where the end of the war postponed its scheduled re-equipment with A-26 Invaders.

Group markings consisted of a white diagonal band (outlined in black on aircraft in natural metal finish) extending from the base of the fin to near the tip of the B-26's rudder. The codes K5, 4T, H9 and 5W were assigned to its 584th through 587th Bombardment Squadrons respectively.

397TH BOMBARDMENT GROUP (MEDIUM)
This group used markings similar to those of the 394th BG (M) but the colour of the diagonal band was yellow instead of white. Its 596th, 587th, 598th and 599th Squadrons applied the codes X2, 9F, U2 and 6B respectively to their Marauders. Flying its first combat mission on 20 April 1944, the 397th BG (M) was the last USAAF B-26 group to be activated, this event taking place on 20 April 1943 at MacDill Field, Florida. The group operated initially from Rivenhall, Essex, but in August 1944 it became the first Ninth Air Force bomb group to be based on the Continent when it was moved to Gorges. It later operated from two other bases in France (Dreux and Péronne) and was based at Venlo, Holland when the war ended. During the Battle of the Bulge the 397th BG (M) was awarded a DUC for cutting the German supply line on 23 December 1943 by hitting the railway bridge at Eller on the Moselle.

409TH BOMBARDMENT GROUP (LIGHT)
Activated at Will Rogers Field, Oklahoma on 1 June 1943, the 409th BG (L) began combat operations on 13 April 1944 from Little Walden, Essex. Equipped with Douglas A-20G and A-20J Havocs the group remained in England until September 1944 when it moved to Bretigny, France. Whilst based there the group converted to A-26 Invaders in time to take part in the Battle of the Bulge with its new aircraft.

Two months later, in February 1945, the group advanced to Laon/Couvron where it remained until it returned to the United States during the summer of 1945. Throughout its thirteen months on operations the 409th BG (L) flew primarily against tactical targets in support of the advance of Gen. Patton's Third Army. Its last mission, however, was flown on 3 May 1945 against an industrial target in Czechoslovakia.

In addition to bearing the squadron codes W5, 7G, D6 and 5I, which respectively identified aircraft from the 640th through 643rd BS, the Havocs and Invaders of the 409th BG were marked with a yellow band, 21in wide, along the length of the trailing edge of the rudder.

410TH BOMBARDMENT GROUP (LIGHT)
Last bomb group to join the Ninth Air Force, the Havoc-equipped 410th was activated at the same time as the 409th BG (L) and flew its first mission on 1 May 1944 from Gosfield. It was immediately active in the pre-invasion operations and went on to support the Normandy landing and Allied advances in Northern France. The group began operating from Coulommiers, France in September 1944 and in February 1945 it moved to Juvincourt. It won a DUC for its participation in the interdiction campaign mounted by the Ninth Air Force in December 1944 to stop the German offensive in the Ardennes. From February 1945 onward and still flying A-20s, some of which had their olive drab and neutral grey camouflage replaced by glossy black paint, the 410th BG (L) increasingly undertook night operations in support of the final campaign in Germany. On 25 April 1944 the group flew its final mission and moved to Beaumont-sur-Oise to be re-equipped with A-26 Invaders.

The markings adopted by the 410th BG (L) were quite colourful and consisted of a white band 21in wide, with three 20in black squares painted on the rudder's trailing edge. From July 1944, its squadrons used not only their assigned codes (5D, 7X, 8U and 6Q) but also painted the cowling lip of their aircraft's engines in different colours (red for the 644th, white for the 645th, blue for the 646th, and yellow for the 647th BS).

416TH BOMBARDMENT GROUP (LIGHT)

The distinguished combat career of this unit, the first light bomber group to join the Ninth Air Force, began on 3 March 1944 when it flew a diversionary mission. The 416th BG (L) then flew several missions against V-1 sites prior to settling down to perform its major function: air support of ground operations. This specialization began on D-Day and continued until the end of the war, the group being particularly active during the breakthrough at St Lô, the reduction of the Falaise gap (during which it earned a DUC), the airborne assault in Holland, the Battle of the Bulge, and the crossing of the Rhine. Whilst taking part in these operations, the 416th BG (L) successively operated from Wethersfield, Essex, and from Melun, Laon/Athies and Cormeilles-en-Vexin, France. Whilst based at Melun the group was re-equipped with A-26s. Group markings were similar to those of the 409th BG (L) but the rudder band was applied in white on camouflaged Havocs and in black on Invaders in natural metal finish.

30. This B-26B-50-MA, 42-95991 of the 37th BS, 17th BG displays—for the sharp-eyed—its red group marking band beneath the tailplane. Further aft than normal, the 17th's band was in fact painted at a point between the side window and the moulded screen of the tail turret. (USAF)

Squadron codes were 5H for the 668th, 2A for the 669th, F6 for the 670th and 5C for the 671st BS.

THE AIRCRAFT

Douglas A-20 Havoc

Classified as an attack aircraft, this twin-engined light bomber traced its origins to a design study undertaken in March 1936 by the Northrop Corporation (then a subsidiary of the Douglas Aircraft Company). A later revision of the design led to the manufacturing of a single prototype, the Douglas 7B, which first flew on 26 October 1938. However, prior to being ordered in production by

31. The 'shark-mouth' identifies this aircraft as belonging to the 444th BS, 320th BG as it lands at Dijon/Longvic, France. The radio call number 2107541 identifies it as a B-26C-45-MO Marauder built by Martin at Omaha, Nebraska. (USAF)

the French Purchasing Commission, the aircraft was extensively redesigned to become the DB-7 which served with the Armée de l'Air and the Royal Air Force.

The model initially ordered by the USAAF was generally similar to the more powerful DB-7A, DB-73 and DB-7B export models powered by 1,600 hp Wright R-2600 radial engines and was designated A-20A in American nomenclature. A few DB-7B Boston IIIs obtained from the RAF were flown in the ETO and North Africa by the 15th BS (L) beginning on 29 June 1942 but the first version of the aircraft flown was the A-20B which was operated by the 47th BG (L) and 68th Observation Group of the Twelfth Air Force. The substantially improved two-seat A-20G and A-20H models with solid nose, housing six forward-firing 0.50in machine guns, and three-seat A-20J and A-20K models with transparent nose, housing a bombardier station and two forward-firing 0.50in machine guns were numerically the most important versions of the Havoc. In Europe they were flown by the 47th BG (L) of the Twelfth Air Force and by the 409th, 410th and 416th BGs (L) of the Ninth Air Force. In addition

to their forward-firing armament, these aircraft were armed with a dorsal turret (twin 0.50in guns) and a ventral 0.50in machine gun and carried between 2,000 and 4,000lb (908 and 1,816kg) of bombs. The A-20Gs and A-20Ks were powered by two 1,600 hp Wright R-2600-23 engines whereas the A-20Hs and A-20Ks and 1,700 hp Wright R-2600-29s.

Including prototypes, export models and 380 aircraft built by Boeing, a total of 7,478 DB-7s and A-20s was built but more than half of these aircraft were delivered, mostly under lend-lease, to the Allies.

Douglas A-26 Invader

Plagued by production delays, the fast Douglas twin-engined bomber needed twenty-eight months after its initial flight to reach its first operational group. By comparison, the much larger and more complex Boeing B-29 Superfortress had required only twenty months between first flight and combat debut. However, the Invader was still operational during most of the Vietnam war whilst the Superfortress had long been retired. Conceived in the autumn of 1940 as a successor to the A-20 which was then about to enter service with the USAAF, the A-26 combined a speed superior to that of its predecessor with the range and offensive load of the larger twin-engined medium bombers such as the B-25 and B-26. Three prototypes were built in the Douglas plant at El Segundo, California, and the XA-26 was first flown on 10 July 1942. Production, however, was assigned to two new Douglas plants located at Long Beach, California and Tulsa, Oklahoma. The initial production plan called for the manufacturing of identical models at both plants, but in 1944 the Long Beach plant was assigned the responsibility for the production of the two-seat A-26B version with solid nose, housing six (later eight) forward-firing 0.50in machine guns whilst the Tulsa plant became responsible for the manufacturing of the three-seat A-26C which had a transparent nose with bombardier station and two forward-firing 0.50in machine guns. Both models also had remotely-controlled dorsal and ventral turrets (each with twin 0.50in guns) and could be fitted with two

twin 0.50in gun packages beneath each wing (later supplanted by three 0.50in guns within each wing). Bombload was 6,000lb (2,722kg). A total of 2,452 Invaders was built by Douglas and the type was first evaluated under combat conditions in New Guinea during July 1944. In Europe, the A-26 fully replaced A-20s and B-26s in the 386th, 391st, 409th and 416th BGs and partially equipped the 410th and 47th BGs (L).

Martin B-26 Marauder
The much maligned and ill-starred B-26 went on from a disheartening combat debut in both the North African and European theatres of operations to gain a solid reputation enhanced by its low loss per sortie ratio. There had been little intrinsically wrong with the Martin medium bomber and proper training and transfer from low-altitude to medium-altitude operations were all that was needed for the USAAF to turn it into one of the truly great aircraft of World War II.

32. Staggering home under the escort of two 432nd BS Marauders, this B-26C-25-MO, 41-35177 of the 34th BS, 17th BG has feathered its port propeller after suffering battle damage. (USAF)

The Marauder was developed in answer to a requirement for a new high-speed medium bomber which had been issued by the Army Air Corps in January 1939, and its prototype was first flown on 25 November 1940. Deliveries of production B-26As began in 1941 and the type was first used to equip the 22nd BG (M). This initial production model was followed in production by the B-26B, B-26C, B-26F and B-26G versions which were built by Martin in its main plant at Baltimore, Maryland, and in a new plant at Omaha, Nebraska. A total of 5,157 Marauders, including prototypes and trainer versions, was built.

In the North African/Mediterranean theatre of operations Marauders equipped the 17th, 319th and 320th BGs (M) of the Twelfth Air Force whilst in the ETO it was flown by the 322nd, 323rd, 344th,

33. **Two Marauders of the 444th BS, 320th BG, 1st Allied Tactical Air Force leave their blazing target—a fuel dump at Collecchio in Italy's Po Valley. (USAF)**

386th, 387th, 391st, 394th and 397th BGs (M) of the Eighth and Ninth Air Forces. Typical of the aircraft flown by these groups was the B-26B which, in its final production forms, carried a defensive armament comprising twelve 0.50in machine guns (one flexible and one fixed gun in the nose, four forward-firing guns in individual blisters on the sides of the forward fuselage, one gun in each waist position, and twin guns in the dorsal and tail turrets) and an offensive load of 4,000lb (1,816kg) of bombs. They were powered by two 2,000 hp Pratt & Whitney R-2800-43 radial engines and were flown by a crew of seven.

North American B-25 Mitchell

In the war against the European Axis powers, the Mitchell equipped only five groups (the 12th, 310th, 321st, 340th and, briefly, 319th BGs) of the Ninth and Twelfth Air Forces in the Western Desert, North Africa and the Mediterranean. None the less, those B-25 groups, made a significant contribution to the Allied war efforts from their debut in the Western Desert when they flew in support of the British Eighth Army during the decisive battle of El Alamein until the last year of the war when they thoroughly disrupted the German retreat in northern Italy.

Designated NA-40, the prototype of a three-seat, twin-engined medium bomber first flew in January 1939, but was destroyed shortly thereafter during its evaluation at Wright Field, Ohio. However, the

34. Impressive line-up of B-26B-20-MA Marauders of an 8th Air Force unit in England. Three groups—the 322nd, 386th and 387th—flew with the 8th AF in 1943.

performance of the experimental aircraft was such that in September 1939, the Army Air Corps placed an initial order for a more powerful development of the aircraft with a wider fuselage, a crew of five and increased gross weight and armament. The first of the new B-25s was flown in August 1940 and the type entered service during the following year with the 17th BG (M). At the start of the war B-25 orders were increased and production of the Mitchell was undertaken not only in the main North American plant at Inglewood, California, where experimental models and B-25A, B, C, G and H production models were built, but also in a plant at Kansas City which built B-25Ds and B-25Js. Total production at both plants was 9,816 aircraft.

During production the Mitchell ·was steadily improved and, whilst the aircraft continued to be powered by a pair of 1,700 hp Wright R-2600 radial engines, its defensive armament was progressively increased. Thus, the last production model, the B-25J, had ten 0.50in machine guns (four forward-firing guns in individual blisters on the fuselage sides, two flexible waist guns, and dorsal and tail turrets with twin guns) plus either one flexible and one fixed 0.50in gun in a transparent bombardier nose or eight 0.50in guns in a solid nose. Normal bombload, however, was only 3,000 lb (1,362 kg). Two models of the Mitchell, the B-25G and B-25H, had a solid nose housing a forward-firing 75mm cannon and, respectively, two and four 0.50in machine guns.

LÉGENDES

1 Douglas A-20B Havoc du 111e Observation Squadron, un unité du Texas National Guard qui pilota des missions de reconnaissance en Afrique du Nord fin 1942. L'insigne de l'escadron est une étoile en or avec un as de carreaux au milieu. **2** La prise d'air au-desses des capots indique que cet avion est un A-20B, 41-3491 du 47e Bomb Group, partageant un terrain d'aviation italien couvert de boue avec des Spitfires (Nos. 93 et 225 Sqns. RAF) et des P-47s (325e Fighter Group). **3** Havoc du 647e BS, 410e BG, 9e Air Force—avec la charge de bombes extérieure. **4** Ce A-20G du 409e BG était baptisé 'La France Libre' lorsqu'il était en poste à Bretigny en Septembre 1944. **5** Formation de A-20G Havocs du 671e BS, 416e BG au-dessus de la France occupée à une altitude de combat typique. **6** La plupart des Havocs avait des nez solides avec des mitrailleuses de 6 × .50; le A-20J avait un nez vitré pour la visée des bombes, et fut utilisé comme un 'chef de peleton des bombardiers'—ici voilà le 410e. BG. **7** A-20J avec un empennage rayé noir et blanc (410e BG) et les rayures blanches du capot et le code '7X' (645e BS). Inaugurées fin de l'été 1944, les rayures du capot, étaient bleues, rouges et jaunes pour les 644e, 646e et 647e respectivement. **8** 'Maxine IV' le A-20J piloté par le commandant du 646e BS, 410e BG, no. 43-9913 codifié 8U-A—notez l'éclair bleu sur le capot du moteur. **9** Les rayures de l'invasion D-Day portées par un A-20J 'Irene', 43-21745, 8U-S du 646e. BS. Les moyeux d'hélices sont probablement bleus. **10 et 11** Des exemples d'emblèmes personnalisés sur le nez d'un avion A-20; 'Suzie' était un A-20K, 44-84 du 410e BG. Le pilote porte L'insigne de reng d'un capitaine.

12 Avion A-26B Invader du 669e. BS, 416e BG, 9th Air Force; ils étaient photographiés quelques temps après que l'unité ait reçu le A-26B en novembre 1944. **13** Avec les portes des bombes ouvertes et des éclats de flak partout; un A-26B du 554e BS, 386e BG au combat le 20 avril 1945. **14** A-26B du 84e BS, 47e BG 12th Air Force, portant curieusement un emblème sur le nez du 118e Tactical Reconnaissance Sqn., qui était à ce moment là avec le 14e Air Force en Chine. **15** A-26Cs arrivés récemment avec le 97e BG en Italie peu de temps après la fin de la guerre européene, toujours dans un mélange de couleurs noir et argent. **16** B-25 Mitchell du 82e BS 12e. BG 9e Air Force au-dessus de l'Afrique du Nord; notez les marques de la RAF sur l'empennage, pour éviter des erreurs. **17** Mitchell bombardiers du 321e BG (des bouts rouges sur l'empennage), 447e BS (blanc 'III'). **18** Mitchells du 487e BS, 340e. BG 12e Air Force affichent une variété de styles différents d'insignes nationaux. **19** Des B-25Js aux empennages noirs du 319e BG. Les numéros d'empennage indiquent les escadrons du 437e (1–24), 438e (25–49), 439e (50–74) et 440e (75–99) respectivement. **20** Avec un 'tableau des raids' de 68 bombes blanches sur le nez, ce B-25 a des rayures jaunes bordées de noir sur l'empennage—la rayure large au-dessus identifie le 310e BG, celle qui est mince en-dessous, le 381e BS. La bande inférieure était blanche, bleue et rouge pour les 379e, 380e et 382e BS respectivement.

21 Mitchells du 340e BG portèrent un code d'empennage de lettres/chiffres. Le chiffre était le dernier unité du numéro de l'escadron (e.g. '6' = 486e BS) et la lettre était une identification individuelle de l'avion. **22** B-26B, 42-43291, du 439e BS, 319e BG laissant tomber des bombes de 1000 livres. **23 et 24** 'Lady Halitosis' un B-26-B Marauder 41-17765 du 17e BG, 12e Air Force après avoir complétés 43 missions rentrant aux USA. **25 et 26** Un autre vétéran du 17e BG—'Hell Cat' du 34e BS avec un groupe de membres de l'équipage d'un B-17e BG posant devant l'appareil. **27** Des bombardiers Marauders du 437e et 440e BS, 319e BG rentrant d'un raid au-dessus de l'Italie. **28** Les derniers seconds d'un Marauders perdu, son moteur tribord complètement enlevé par du flak au-dessus de Toulon. **29** Des détails de la réserve de bombes et des positions inférieures des canons d'un Marauder au-dessus de l'Italie. **30** B-26B Marauder d'un 37e BS 17e BG, la rayure rouge autour du fuselage arrière, qui identifiait ce groupe, est à peine visible en-dessous de l'empennage.

31 L'emblème des 'dents du requin' indique que ce Marauder volait avec le 444e BS, 320e BG, la photo montre un 2107451 atterrissant à Dijon/Longvic France. **32** Avec un moteur endommagé, un 41-35177 du 34e BS, 17e BG rentre en chancelant assisté par deux autres Marauders du 432e BS. **33** B-26 Marauders du 444e BS, 320e BG (photographiés avant l'introduction des 'dents de requin') par dessus un dépôt d'essence en flammes à Collechio dans la Vallée du Po. **34** B-26 Marauders D'un des groupes de Marauders du 8e Air Force—le 322e, 386e ou 387e BG, roulent sur un terrain d'aviation anglais en 1943.

Notes sur les planches en couleurs

Page 25 : Capitain, pilote, US 9th Air Force, 1944, en tenue de jour et casquette verte olive et les pantalons 'soi-disant' roses. L'attribut doré, national sur la casquette. Des insignes US sur les deux revers supérieurs, des insignes Air Force sur les deux revers inférieurs; un attribut de pilote au-dessus de la poche de poitrine à gauche; des insignes du 9th Air Force sur l'épaule gauche seulement; des galons de rang d'un 'Captain' sur les épaulettes. La rayure de ganse foncée autour des poignets était portée par du personnel officier seulement.

Page 26 en haut : Douglas A-20B Havoc du 84e BS, 47e BG à Souk-el-Arba, Tunisie, mai 1943. Notez les hublots du nez couverts de peinture—l'avion a été équipé de canons supplémentaires au nez; le '9' est le numéro d'idendité individuel de l'avion; le chiffre d'appel/radio sur l'empennage est selon le mode américaine, le numéro de série sans le premier numéro—(4) 1-3272. Le nom 'Tutu' et le panneau d'étoiles jaunes des raids étaient ajoutés par l'équipage. Les couleurs sont réglementaires Olive Drab et Neutral Gray. **Page 26 en bas :** Par contraste, une combinaison de couleurs plutôt britannique sur le B-25C, 42-32529, du 488e BS, 340e BG, 9e Air Force à Sfax, Tunisie en mai 1943. Les couleurs sont Desert Pink peints par dessus avec des rayures Olive Drab et Neutral Gray. L'emblème RAF de l'empennage est porté. Sur l'empennage, '8' indique l'escadron et 'S' l'avion individuel.

Page 27 : Douglas A-20K Havoc du 645e BS, 410e BG 9e Air Force à Juvincourt, France février 1945. L'avion est peint en noir brillant, mais il a un gouvernail de recharge camouflé en Olive Drab et Medium Green. Le '7X' et la rayure blanche du capot indique l'escadron; notez le lavis gris clair sur le fuselage et les insignes des ailes, et le nom 'Helen' sur le nez—Les capots du moteur sont très marqués par des gaz d'échappement.

Pages 28, 29: B-26B Marauder du 444e BS, 320e BG à Dijon/Longvic, France, début 1945. La gueule et les yeux d'un requin, assortis à la forme du nez, sont un motif des l'escadron. Fini en Olive Drab et Neutral Gray, la combinaison réglementaire de colours, l'avion porte une rayure jaune de 10 pouces autor du fuselage arrière comme un emblème de groupe, et un numéro jaune individuel 'de bataille' et le signe d'appel radio sur l'empennage.

Page 30: Douglas A-26C Invader, 43-22641, du 574e BS, 391e BG 9e Air Force à Asse Belgique en avril 1945. Les codes '4L8 et 'V' se réfèrent à l'escadron et l'avion individuel respectivement, et les marques jaunes et noires sur l'empennage se réfèrent au groupe.

Page 31 en haut: Insignes individuels (1) Les marques sur le nez et l'empennage du B-25C du 83e BS, 12e BG à Medenine, Tunisie, printemps 1943. Aucune autre marque à part les insignes nationaux, étoiles blanches sur des disques bleus en six positions. (2) B-26B du 554e BS, 386e BG à Boxted, Angleterre, 1943–44. L'appel radio 131877 en jaune sur l'empennage; et une large rayure horizontale en jaune pardessus; des codes rouges ternes 'RU-V' sur le fuselage; des insignes nationaux étoiles et barres en six positions. (3) Côté bâbord du nez, et des marques assorties sur l'empennage d'un B-25C d'un unité inconnue. Des insignes nationaux, d'étoiles sur disques bordés de jaune. (4) L'emblème du nez tribord du même avion photographié plus tard, à ce moment là la barre jaune avait disparu de l'empennage ainsi que les bordures jaunes des insignes nationaux. **Page 31 en bas:** Model 969A camion grue sur un chassis 4 ton 6 × 6 Diamond T utilisé sur des terrains d'aviation USAAF pour du travail imprévu.

Page 32 à gauche: Technical Sergeant: US 12e Air Force en tenue de sortie, en region Méditerranéene 1943–44. Cet uniforme léger des tropiques—'chinos'—était porté avec un calot du même tissus, gansé des colours de l'Armée de l'Air, orange et bleu. Des chevrons de rang sur les deux manches; les insignes de l'épaule gauche des Forces de l'Armée et de l'Air. **Page 32 à droite:** Lieutenant, équipage US 9e Air Force 1944, calot vert olive avec de la ganse dorée et noir et l'insigne de rang accroché au côté gauche; pantalons de tenue de jour vert olive, et un pullover de laine vert olive. Le blouson de pilote en cuir à fermeture éclair a des épaulettes, un écusson 9e Air Force sur l'épaule gauche, et un petit nom peint sur la poitrine. Les bottes de pilote sont réglementaires, Type A-6.

ÜBERSCHRIFT

1 Douglas A-20B Havoc of 111th Observation Squadron, eine Texas National Guard Einheit die für Aufklärungszwecke, spät im jfahre 1942 in Nordafrika eingesetzt wurde. Das Staffelemblem ist ein goldene Stern mit dem As-Karo als Herzschild. **2** A-20B; Kennzeichendie Kühlungsluftöffnungen oben auf den Motorhauben. Dieses Flugzeug, 41-3491, der 47th Bomb Group, teilt seinen schlammigen italienischen Flugplatz mit Spitfires (Nos 93 & 225 Sqns. RAF) und P-47s (325th Fighter Group). **3** Havoc vom 647th BS. 410th BG, 9th Air Force mit aussenangebrachten Bomben. **4** Eine Gruppe A-20G Havocs vom 671st BS, 416th BG über deutschbesetzten Europa in Typischer Einsatzhöhe. **5** Dieses A-20G der 409th BG wurde 'La France Libre'

zu Bretigny, September 1944 getauft. **6** Grundsätzlich hatten Havocs massive Rumpfspitzen mit 6 × .50 M-Gs; das A-20J war aber mit einer Rumpfspitze aus Glas, um den Bombenrichter platz zu geben, ausgestattet. Diese Flugzeuge, wie hier mit der 410th Bg, wurden als Bomber 'Leithammel' eingesetzt. **7** A-20J mit schwarz-weisse Schwanzfloss streifen (410th BG), weisse Motorhaubestreifen und Erkennungsmarke '7X' (645th BS). Die Motorhaubestreifen wurden in Spätsommer 1944 eingeführt. Und waren rot (644th BS), blau (646th BS) und gelb (647th BS). **8** 'Maxine IV', die A-20J des Kommandeur, 646th BS, 410th BG, Nummer 43-9913, Erkennungsbuchstaben: 8U-A. Die blaue Motorhaubestreife beachten! **9** D-Day Invasion Erkennungsstreifen auf A-20J 'Irene', 43-21745, 8U-S des 646th BS. Der Propeller-Knauf war wahrscheinlich blau gestrichen. **10 & 11** Einige Beispiell persönliche Rumpfspitzenembleme auf A-20 Flugzeuge: 'Suzie', eine A-20K, 44-84 der 410th BG. Der Pilot trägt die Dienstgrandabzeichen eines Hauptmannes.

12 A-26B Invader-maschinen vom 669th BS, 416th BG, 9th Air Force. Das Bild wurde November 1944, kurz nach der Übernahme die A-26B von dieser Einheit. **13** A-26B von 554th BS, 386th BG von FLA detonationen umringt und mit geöffneten Bombenschachttüren während einem Einsatzflug am 20 April 1945. **14** Eine A-26B vom 84th BS, 47th BG, 12th Air Force. Merkwurdigeweise trägt die Maschine das Rumpfspitzenemblem des 118th Tactical Reconnaisance Squadron, der damals mit der 14th Air Force in China im Einsatz war. **15** Diese A-26Cs, neulich beim 97th BS, 47th BG in Italien kurz nach dem Kriegsende in Europa angeflogen, tragen noch den schwarzsilverne Anstrich. **16** B-25 Mitchell vom 82nd BS, 12th BG, 9th Air Force über Nordafrika. Die RAF Schwanzflossmarkierung—extra Schutz gegen Identifizierungsfehlerbeachten. **17** Mitchell Bomber der 321st BG (rote Schwanzflossspitzen), 447th BS (weisse 'III'). **18** Mitchells der 487th BS, 340th BG, 12th Air Force mit verschiedenen Ausführungen von Hoheitsemblemen. **19** Schwarzschwänzige B-25Js der 319th BG. Die Schwanz-nummern bedeuten: (1–24) 437th; (25–49) 438th; (50–74) 439th and (75–99) 440th Staffel. **20** Diese B-25 hat einen Lufteinsatztafel mit 68 weisse Bomben und an den Schwanzfloss schwarzumrandete gelbe Streifen: oben (breit) heisst 310th BG; unten (schmal)—381st BS. Die unterste Streife war weiss (379th BS), blau (380th BS) oder rot (382 BS). **21** Mitchells von der 340th BG waren durch eine Buchstabe/Nummer Chiffer auf dem Schwanzfloss identifiziert. Die Nummer war die letzte Nummer der Staffel nummer (z.B 6' = 486th BS), die Buchstabe war die Flugzeug erkennungsmarke. **22** B-26B, 42-43291, vom 439th BS, 319th BG beim Absetzen 1,000lb Bomben. **23 & 24** 'Lady Halitosis' eine B-26B Marauder, 41-17765 der 17th BG 12th Air Force. Nach 43 Einsätze ist sie auf der Heimflug nach Amerika. **25 & 26** Noch ein Veteran der 17th BG—'Hell Cat' vom 34th BS. Im Vordergrund einige Bordbesatzungsmitglieder von der 17th BG. **27** Marauder Bomber der 437th und 440th BS auf den Heimweg nach einen Einsatz über Italien. **28** Die letzen Sekunden einer Marauder; ihre steuerbord Motor wurde von der Fla über Toulon weggeschossen. **29** Innenbild eines Marauders Bombenschacht und untere M-G Schützenstelle. Über Italien. **30** B-26B Marauder vom 37th BS, 17th BG. Die Erkennungsmarke dieser Gruppe, eine rote Streife um den Rumpfhinterteil, ist gerader unter dem Schwanz sichtbar.

31 Nach dem Hai-schnauze Emblem gehört diese Marauder dem 444th BS, 320th BG. Das Bild zeigt Flugzeug Nummer 2107451 bei einer Landung in Dijon/Longvic, Frankreich. **32** Mit beschädigten Motor, hinkt diese Maschine, 41-35177 vom 34th BS, 17th BG, vom zwei anderen Marauders (vom 432nd BS) begleitet, nach Hause. **33** B-26 Marauders vom 444th BS, 320th BG im Einsatz über einen brennenden Treibstofflager bei Collechio im Potal. Das Bild wurde vor der Einführung des Hai-Schnauze Emblems gemacht. **34** B-26B Marauders einer der 8th Air Force Marauder Gruppen—hier 322nd, 386th oder 387th BG fahren zum Starten, England 1943.

Farbtafeln

Seite 25: Captain Pilot, US 9th Air Force, 1944, in olivgrüner Jacke und Mütze und die sogennanten 'rosaroten' Hosen. Goldene, amerikanische Mützenemblem, 'US' auf beiden oberen Kragenspitzen, Air Force Abzeichen auf den unteren Kragenspitzen. Über die linke Brusttasche des Fliegerabzeichen, 9th Air Force Emblem nur auf der linken, Dienstgradabzeichen auf beiden Schulterklappen. Nur Offiziere trugen die dunkelen Armelstrifen.

Seite 26 (Oben): Douglas A-20B Havoc vom 84th BS, 47th BG, Sonk-el-Arba, Tunesien, Mai 1943. Das Flugzeug ist mit zusätzlichen Rumpfspitzen M-Gs ausgerüstet worden, deshalb die Überstrichenen Fensterscheiben. Die '9' ist die Flugzeugnummer; auf den Seitensteuerfläche ist die Flugzeugfunksprechsignatur, wie bei den Amerikanern üblich, die Flugzeugnummer mit dem ersten Ziffer entfernt-(4) 1-3272. Die Name 'Tutu' und die Siegestafel mit den gelben Sternen waren von der Besatzungmitglieder angebracht. Die Farben sind Olive Drab und Neutral Gray. **Seite 26 (Unten):** Als Gegenstück ein Flugzeug B-25C, 42-32529 vom 488th BS, 340th BG, 9th Air Force, bei Sfax, Tunesien, Mai 1943, in 'britischen' Farben. Der Anstrich ist Desert Pink mit Olive Drab und Neutral Gray zusatzstreifen. Das RAF Seitensteueremblem ist auch zu sehen; die Schwanznummer '8' deutet auf den Staffel hin; 'S' ist die Flugzeugerkennungsbuchstabe.

Seite 27: Eine Douglas A-20K Havoc vom 645th BS, 410th BG, 9th Air Force bei Juvincourt, Frankreich, Fevruar 1945. Die Maschine hat einen glanzschwarzen Anstrich ausser der Ersatz Seitensteuerfläche, die Olive Drab und Medium Green noch angestrichen ist. Staffelerkennungsmarken: '7X' und die weisse Motorenhaubestreife. Die hellgraue überschicht zu den Rumpf

und Flugelemblemen und die Name 'Helen' an der Rumpfspitze beachten! Die Motorenhauben sind durch die Auspuffgase diskoloriert worden.

Seiten 28, 29: B-26B Marauder vom 444th BS, 320th BG, Dijon/Longvic, Frankreich im Frükling 1945. Staffelemblem—die Hai-Schnauze an der Rumpfspitze; Gruppenemblem—die 10 inch gelbe Streife um den Rumpfhinterteil. Das Flugzeug führt eine gelbe 'Schlachtennummer' und Funksprechsignatur auf der Seitensteuerfläche und hat das Farbenschema Olive Drab und Neutral Gray.

Seite 30: Douglas A-26C Invader, 43-22641 vom 574th BS, 391st BG, 9th Air Force, Asse, Belgien, April 1945. Staffelmarke—'4L'; Flugzeugbuchstabe—'V'; Gruppenmarke—gleb-schwarze Schwanzteile.

Seite 31 (Oben): Flugzeug-Marken (1) Rumpfspitzenund Schwanzmarkierungen einer B-25C vom 83rd BS, 12th BG, Medenine, Tunesien, Frühling 1943. Sie trägt keine andere Embleme ausser der National-Kokardenweisse Sterne auf blauen Rundkreisen in sechs Stellen. (2) B-26B vom 554th BS, 386th BG, Boxted, England 1943–44. Funksprechsignatur: 131877 in gelbe auf der Seitensteuerfläche, darüber breite, waagerechte gelbe Streife. Dunkelrote 'RU-V' an der Rumpfseite; National-Kokarden (Sterne und Balken) in sechs Stellen. (3) Backbordseite der Rumpfspitze und Seitensteuerfläche einer B-25C einer unbekannten Einheit. National-Kokarden. Sterne auf Rundkreisen mit gelber Umrandung. (4) Die selbe Maschine (das Bild wurde von der Steuerbordseite und etwas später gemacht). Die gelbe Schwanz flossstreife und die Kokardenumrandungen sind schon weg. **Seite 31 (Unten):** USAAF Bergungslastwagen: 4 ton 6 × 6, Diamond T' LKW mit model 969A Kran aufgebaut.

Seite 32 (Links): Technical Sergeant, US 12th Air Force in Ausgehanzug, Mittelmeergebiet 1943–44. Zu dieser Tropenuniform—'chinos' gehörte ein Schiffchen aus demselben Stoff mit Vorstoss in blau und orange. Dienstgradabzeichen auf beiden Ärmeln; links das Wappen der Heeresluftwaffen. **Seite 32 (Rechts):** Lieutenant, Bordbesatzung, US 9th Air Force, 1944. Schiffchen mit schwarz und goldenem Offiziersvorstoss und Dienstgradabzeichen. Olivgrünem Hosen und Woll-Pullover. Die Lederne Fliegerjacke mit Reissverschluss hat Dienstgradabzeichen auf den Schulterklappen, 9th Air Force Wappen an den linken Oberarm und eine Spitzname vorne angestrichen Die Fliegerstiefel sind Vorschriftsmässig, Typ A-6.